Flora Tristan,

A Forerunner Woman

Magda Portal
Second edition

Order this book online at www.trafford.com
or email orders@trafford.com

Most Trafford titles are also available at major online book retailers.

Editor Renée Castro-Pozo,
my e-mail HYPERLINK "mailto:reneec_p@yahoo.ca" reneec_p@yahoo.ca
and phone number, 416-2567322

Printed in the United States of America.

ISBN: 978-1-4669-3414-6 (sc)
ISBN: 978-1-4669-3416-0 (hc)
ISBN: 978-1-4669-3415-3 (e)

Library of Congress Control Number: 2012908154

Trafford rev. 05/09/2012

 www.trafford.com

North America & international
toll-free: 1 888 232 4444 (USA & Canada)
phone: 250 383 6864 ♦ fax: 812 355 4082

EDITOR'S NOTE TO THE FIRST EDITION

Our dream became reality with the publication of this book, and the fact that it is in your hands today.

We are the six women who have worked as a team, with different ages and professions: Magda Portal; Otilia Navarrete; Sonia Canales; Elena Quiñe de Delgado; Carmen Castro Pozo de Urteaga; and Renée Castro-Pozo. We are united by our pressing desire to bring knowledge to women through literature, a medium that urgently needs it due to high illiteracy rates and illiteracy from disuse. In our country, the most unimaginable forms of sub-literature proliferate. We are confronting this enemy and, though we know our undertaking is not easy, we are determined to surmount all difficulties.

Through the author's diligent research, the union of Flora Tristan and Magda Portal overcomes a century of difference, giving us an important work on the great forerunner of Feminist ideology.

We pay homage in admiration of Flora Tristan who, ahead of her time and with a clear mind, perceived class struggles and proposed worker's union. She also saw the potential in women, who were drowsy from oppression and hounded by economic anguish and daily survival. In order to achieve their Freedom and Equality, Tristan demanded the participation of women at all levels and instances.

Therefore, we respectfully remember a poem by the Pariah that evokes with realism the need to unite and organize ourselves for a just world! Uníos! !Uníos!.

LET'S UNITE, UNITE!

If, yes, we will unite so that our daughters
Do not dishonor home by selling themselves from hunger,
So that hope shines on our families
So that our elders can have their bread.

Yes, yes, we will unite and each one
Will contribute a brave heart to our militia
So that finally, they will yield legitimately to us
The most precious gift: the right to work.

Yes, yes, we will unite so that misery
Does not pin crowns of pain to our foreheads,
So that if our arms fertilize the earth
We receive the joy of harvesting the flower.

Yes, yes, we will unite but without curses
It hurts our frank lips to curse,
We do not want fires, hatred or destruction,
We only want to: Construct! Construct!

!Unite! Unite!

2a English version

Yes, yes, we will unite so that our daughters
Don't sell them short, dishonouring home
So those hope shines in our families,
So that our elders may have bread.

Yes, yes, we will unite so that each one
May bring to our military a brave heart
So that they can concede, with justice at last,
The right to work; the most precious gift of all.

Yes, yes, we'll unite so that misery
Doesn't crown our temples with wreaths of pain,
And that if our own arms work the fields
We will have the joy of harvesting the flower.

Yes, yes, we will unite but without rancor.
From our lips no curses poison truth.
We don't want firestorms, hatred or destruction,
We want only to construct, to construct.

—0—

Renée Castro-Pozo March, 1983
First Edition

Sonia
Canales

Otilia
Navarrete

Renée
Castro Pozo

Elena Quiñe

Magda Portal

Carmen Flora
C.P. de Urteaga

Initial Group Editorial La Equidad

PREFACE TO THE SECOND EDITION IN ENGLISH ABOUT MAGDA PORTAL

Before I met Magda Portal, I already knew about her. At home, my father always had commented about the political parties, and Magda Portal always stuck out as the founder of APRA—Popular Revolutionary American Alliance—which main tenet was anti-imperialism. He related how in the Lima's large rallies or in the provinces, people greeted the leaders with their call: "Victor Raul, Magda Portal!" popular saying as a victory call, and a tribute to this great combative woman who was the leader in her time.

Magda Portal Moreno was born in Barranco district, Lima, Peru, on May 27th of 1900. She belonged to a middle class before her father died and the family was apart. She began to successfully express herself using poetry. She won a series of writing awards at an early age. At the age of twenty three years old, won her first literary prize *"La Flor Natural"—"The Natural Flower"—at the Universidad Nacional Mayor de San Marcos' en los Juegos Florales—Floral Games,—with her poems collection "Anima Absorta".*

As a consequence to her political activism, and desire for social revolution for the oppressed, was exiled to Mexico and Chile. In 1924, in Mexico, she became the cofounder of APRA and formed part of the team of directors.

Initially, APRA seems to have the same goals of social change that Magda had, and she was appointed the Minister of Women Affairs. But by 1948, she realized that the party was not fulfilling its original mandate, so she left the party along with other women associates. There is a very interesting dialogue that happened at a national political convention between Magda and the party's cofounder: Victor Raul Haya de la Torre. He was as well her former political colleague.

He announced that women should be excluded from National Executive Committee meetings because they didn't have rights to vote. The exchange went like this:

—Victor Raul Haya de la Torre. We have arrived at the conclusion that since women can't vote in Peru, they can't be considered actual members of the aprista party; women can only be supporters.

—Magda Portal: Pido la palabra!—I request the floor!-

—Haya de la Torre: No hay nada en debate.—There is nothing to debate-.

—Magda Portal: I request the floor!

—Haya de la Torre: No hay nada en debate.

—Magda Portal: !Esto es fascismo!—This is fascism!—

Two years later, Magda Portal is on a CIA list of dissidents.

This event gave way to hard retaliation from her ex-party members against her. There were attempts against her life, her car was put on fire, and with their influence she lost her job as representative of Fondo de Cultura Economica of Mexico in Lima.

I know many first hand anecdotes. One time, when the apristas were persecuted by the government of Sanchez Cerro, in the 1930s, Magda, trying to escape the city was not able to secure a hiding place, and had to spend the night in a ditch, out in the open country surrounded by critters large and small. In the face of danger, she had to stay on watch all night long.

As a result of her opposition to the dictatorship she was imprisoned in 1934 for 500 days in the Santo Tomas Jail, which was the women's detention Centre until 1950. Two years later this prison was converted into the "Gran Unidad Escolar Mercedes Cabello de Carbonera" women's high school.

In 1968, she received a special mention for her poems collection "La Constancia del Ser",—"The Being's Constancy"—. Her beautiful poems have been translated to English, Bulgarian and French.

Magda was a participant of "Penguin Book of Women Poets" in London, 1979. In 1980, was invited to the IV Congress of Women Writers.

In 1981, she was given a Lifetime Achievement Award at the International Women's Conference. From there she travelled to U.S.A. invited by the Universities of Lexington, Kentucky, Austin, and Berkeley. Her name was engraved in a grand obelisk together with other notable literary figures.

In the 80s, very difficult times for Peru, she successfully led the "Writers and Artists National Association"—ANEA—She surrounded herself with notables in the sciences and arts due to the essential nature of the association, which was created in 1938, same year of Cesar Vallejo's death.

She recovered the institution's prestige, and lifted it to new high levels. She made sure the association was always on the people's side, leader to social struggle, committed to international solidarity.

Magda's moral standards were very strict; her ethical stature was undeniable. She did not allowed sex or drinking excesses in the institution, which happened on prior administrations. She led the association with the propriety of her action.

I see a parallel between those two great but little—known Western revolutionary figures:

Tristan from 19ᵗʰ century France, and Portal from 20ᵗʰ century Peru.

Both were pioneers in their struggles to improve the plight of the oppressed through political activism.

Both spread their ideas with speaking tours and publications that were highly influential in their times.

Both challenged the status quo to such an extent that each was classified as "a threat to the state".

Both were born in opulent families but when her father died they became poor, and thrown onto the streets by creditors.

Both put emphasis in condemn prostitution as the most horrific of the plagues that inequality on the world's resources distribution yields. This infamy withers the human species and attempts against the social organization even more than crime.

Both were persecuted for the police when they defend the poor people.

Both had very bad marriages and suffered personal distress.

Our groups of feminists were very proud to have her as our torch bearer. Many of our meetings took place at the ANEA's quarters.

APRA, the political party came to power for the first time in 1980-1985. Some young aprista leaders, who were sent by the president and political chief, came to her residence in Miraflores expressing their interest to have her back in the ranks of the party, and offering her a good job opportunity. To their proposition she answered proudly: "Yo avanzo, no retrocedo", "I advance; I do not move backwards".

It was never in her plans to go back to that treacherous and corrupted political party that had broken its primary tenets.

Magda was actively working on the consolidation of the great Flora Tristan's research, whose works she was introduced to initially in Chile at the time of her exile. Right there and then she decided to convert her research into a book. In addition, I projected to start a women's

EDITORIAL for women. Many established publishing houses offered Magda to publish her work, but since we were such close friends, and she was aware of my proposed enterprise in favor of women, she agreed to be part of the initial editorial group. I named the women's publisher that would print books for women: EQUALITY.

The whole process of "Flora Tristan Precursor" was done by Magda and I side by side. As Magda toiled on her typewriter, I would organize the typed pages on long lengths of paper as pre-setting for printing. Magda was so pleased with my work, that it was expressed in her dedication note on my 45th birthday:

"To Renée Castro, author of "Flora Tristan" on her day, with sincere friendship. Magda Portal, April 13, 1983.

In 1984, Magda also attended the "Premier Colloque Flora Tristan, un Fabuleux Destin" in Dijon, France. From there she visited the URSS and other important European cities.

A short time later, I accompany her to a notary to change the ownership deed of the apartment, which she and her only sister shared, to her sister's name. This proved to be a very good precautionary measure to protect her younger half-sister.

Magda suffered the loss of her memory and other intellectual faculties long before she was declared a victim to Alzheimer disease. She was exhausted, and had lost the desire to live. She talked about euthanasia, about the best way to go without having to endure so much grief and sorrow. She only allowed her sister to visit, the doctors and myself. Magda had, signed; in advance, consenting forms to be cremated. We searched all over Lima for neurology specialists; the best ones coming from Hospital Obrero—Worker's Hospital—Grau Avenue. These doctors were very supportive and caring to the end.

On a commonly grey Lima's afternoon on July 11 of 1989, we held the wake in the Parque Universitario of the Universidad Nacional Mayor de San Marcos, where she had, as a young woman, won the "Juegos Florales" with her beautiful and immortal poetry.

RENEE CASTRO de CASTRO—POZO
2012

ACKNOWLEDGMENTS

I think English is a difficult language, to translate a book is also an expensive and big task. After some time living in Canada, I realized that Flora Tristan wasn't known by English readers men or women here.

I had luck when Carmela Valles introduce me to Rita Granda, M.A. in Spanish from the University of Toronto, and professional translator from York University. She read the book in Spanish, and she fell in love with the subject, the author Magda Portal, and Flora.

We started the translation of the book "Flora Tristan Precursora" which I published in Lima—Peru in 1983 under Editorial La Equidad, House Publisher I founded along with five more women.

In Peterborough, we went to different venues to talk about Flora Tristan, and nobody knew who was that Peruvian—French woman. That was an incentive to continue working in the translation.

There were very good friends supporting my goal, to put this book about Flora Tristan, a great personality forerunner of her time, in the hands of English readers.

I could mention:

Cheryl Lyon, Margaret Slavin, Stephanie Benn, Rob Steinman, Loredana Crina Iacome, Pete Hewett, Karen Hjort-Jensen, Ziysah Markson, Carmela Valles, Carol Winter, Kathryn Langley, Teresa Good, Prof. Andreas Pickel, Jo Hayward-Haines, Elizabeth Aguilar, Candy Reyes and Gina Emberly.

Special thanks to my daughter Talia Castro-Pozo C. for her enormous intellectual and financial support. To the New Canadians Centre for gave me the space to meet our friends in cultural and artistic activities.

I was finishing this project with a friend and poet I met in Toronto when we came to listen to beautiful poetry sessions, Enrique Castro, he deserves my deep thanks.

And always my love to my husband Pepe for his sharp ideas and the significant support of my son Ph-D Tristan D. Castro-Pozo C.

RENEE C. CASTRO-POZO
2012

D'après A.-L. Constant: *Les Belles Femmes de Paris*

"FLORA WAS ADMIRED IN THE 1837, 1838, 1839 ANNUAL EXHIBITION, IN THE PARIS MOST BEAUTIFUL WOMEN SALON" PAINTER JULES LAURE

Dedicated to the women of Peru with my faith in their future free from submission.

Magda Portal

AUTHOR'S NOTE

Flora Tristan's name became known to me based on the version by Ventura García Calderón in his book "A Peru is Worth it", Paris 1939 in which he dedicates one of his essays titled "Nuestra Santa Aventurera"—"Our Blessed Adventurer". His beautiful prose is almost a poem but his tone is so saturated with compliments as it deals with a social fighter, it left me with an acid taste. Nevertheless, it was my first contact with the Precursor and it was worth the trouble. But something drew my attention in his story. He said about her: "Flora Tristan's reputation of being the forerunner of the International Worker had a detrimental effect". [1]

However, other books existed outside of Peru that cited, discussed and identified her without greater significance. Few gave her here fair impact among the first movements of social demands that dawned then in Europe and of

---

[1]   Ventura G. C. "Vale un Perú". Paris, 1939. Pp. 152-162

which Flora is an authentic instigator. In Chile and during my 4—and—a-half-year exile in that country, where I was able to learn more about this unique woman, I was invited by the Mujeres Socialistas, Socialist Women, to their first conference, requesting of me a lecture called: "Flora Tristan, Precursor", which shows that the women of Chile did have knowledge of the life and work of Flora and wanted more information from a Peruvian woman.

Obviously, I had to research in encyclopedic dictionaries and even in the Encyclopedia Brittanica, for news of the fighter, which certainly wasn't much given the ominous silence to which she was still relegated by them.

From this first essay written in Chile, in 1944, we published a new edition not proofread in 1945 at my return to Peru.

This tardy third edition—because Flora's name and her work had conquered its place in history therefore, in all bookstores in Paris and the world—had been extended by the contribution of many of my researchers and the collaboration of many of my girlfriends who lived outside of Peru, without changing the original content. This work wishes to be more than a meticulous investigation, a vindication of the very being of the women and the fighter that Flora Tristan was. Collecting data, and quotes from the book itself "Workers Union", last edition of the Publishing House Fontamara S.A. of Barcelona, 1977.

Translating from the French by Yolanda Marco, is the first edition in Spanish and her translator kept a magnificent loyalty to the thought of the author, glossing the text and reaffirming her promising concepts, without increasing or decreasing the fervent expressions and extraordinary in their approach, dedicated to convince to the working class of the need to unite to confront the fight against the exploitation and misery hanging over them.

It is important and necessary not to forget that the "Workers Union" maintains from the outset of its creation, the vindication of the woman as irreversible premise, just like Flora said: "without liberation of the woman there will be not liberation of the man"

INTRODUCTION

INTERNATIONAL WOMEN'S YEAR
QUANTITIVE BALANCE

"The degree of women's emancipation is a measure
of a society's emancipation"

Charles Fourier,
19ᵗʰ Century

The proclamation of International Women's Year
in 1975, which later became the "Women's Decade",
instituted by the United Nations, constituted a unique
event by the intrinsic meaning of its content having in it
the denunciation that women have not formed an integral
part of the Woman-Man couple; that recently her rights
have been recognized as the result of the tenacious and
permanent fight of a substantial sector of women who
for many years pursue equality in the human couple,
demanding their privileges and claiming not to continue

only complying with the function imposed by nature to continue the species. With the exception of women from the socialist countries in which women occupy their place in the social group on a par with men, in the rest of the civilized and underdeveloped world, equality has not been reached yet that the feminine sex seeks, maintaining many of the old prejudices that frequently women themselves contribute to the reinforcement, accepting supremacy of men in the home, in society and in work, whether it be for indecision, ignorance or convenience.

Despite these arguments, women's emancipation is taking place without large frontal attacks, only pushed by the times that we live in when no one yields their place, whether they are weak or strong, woman or man. This revolution is produced mainly by the work of the youth who are anxious to eliminate the old perceptions of the domestic woman, creating a unisex girl, ready to defend her vital space in the advance towards the recuperation of everything that she is competed with and that our grandmothers and mothers undoubtedly dreamed of.

Those exceptional women who distinguished themselves years ago with their anti-discriminatory arrests or those who gave themselves to political or patriotic struggles defending their people's independence, make up a minority that have been taken into account only in an anecdotal way the same as they were exceptional. Nevertheless, there were many and History has recorded the names of some of those who did not hesitate to offer their lives for a cause that they felt was just. Many did not demand nor receive reward.

Among them, the 'Sufragettes' who fought real battles to obtain women's rights to vote, which was an obligatory step, according to them, in order to achieve equality with men. They were wounded and humiliated and their attempts were ridiculed. But they are in the memories, and are recognized by those who later would not forget this exalted example of woman's character.

There are many women who wrote their names in History demanding their rights as the diminished sex, like minors. But it is important for Women's Liberation to clear up the activities and life of one of the women who flourished in the first half of the past century and who was a true torch for illuminating awareness without hating men and continuing to be an authentic woman.

From there, in accordance with this preface, she can be found among the social fighters of greater hierarchy, the precursor of women's liberation who, without anti-male confrontations co-existed with the awakening social movements that were incubating in this period, place emphasis on the review of the tremendous injustices weighing upon women, demanding for her not only the elimination of the laws that diminish her, placing her in a situation of permanent dependence on man, but had subjected her to infamous conditions of feudal origins, endorsed by tradition and religion.

And it is necessary to honour her also as a Peruvian fighter, as member of the community of this part of the world that is Peru, where her father was born and to which she felt linked, calling the Peruvians her 'compatriots'.

That is why in homage to the women who continue to struggle, who more and more strip themselves of prejudices and fears in order to gain access to the fullest balance of the human couple, who have achieved already many conquests with great effort, I wish to highlight the notable Peruvian-French fighter, FLORA TRISTAN.

THE WOMEN'S SITUATION IN PERU

I consider it a duty to expose in this preface the actual status of women in Peru, though brief, up to where she shows herself in her diverse vital connotations and within the technological advancements and great socio-political changes.

I believe that I am not mistaken in saying that the vast majority of women in Peru continue to be relegated to the situation of minors, under male guardianship and subject to restrictions that **coerce** her liberty, yielding to the imposition of obsolete laws that impede them from discovering new horizons that could raise her level within society. Her identification is revealing: "Profession: Housewife", which define her by the limits of her existence as being solely dedicated to the obligation of serving in the home, caring for children and the husband within conventional activities.

Nevertheless, it should be pointed out there exists a good percentage of women of legal age who have achieved the breaking of obstacles and prejudices that tie them to ignorance, leisure and conformity. It is obvious that at this time, all of the education centers—universities, academies, colleges, etc.—are populated by girls, who invade their classrooms with the desire to broaden in their knowledge, as per their economic abilities, since the State does not promote free higher level studies nor any other than primary school.

If the class based society in which we find ourselves, stimulated the many young women, anxious to continue their studies, it would be easy to note that they make up more than 50 % of the female students and that most of them finish their studies and find a place in professional institutions, although they are not offered the best positions.

But in Peru, it isn't just the capital city. Our country with its 25 departments, with a population close to 20 million of which 51 % are women, [1] still determines the normal development of the feminine element, under pressure by the demands they face in the struggle for life without relying on the protection of the **farsighted** State.

---

[1] Now, 2012, the population is 28'220,764 hab. 50. 3 % women = 13'789,517

The provinces lack the facilities that the capital can offer and although in the main departments there are universities because of the population and economic abilities, these are not as complete as in the capital, from whence comes the exodus of most of the students. Generally, the provincial girls reach middle studies and for economic reasons, they are not able to gain access to upper education. From there, family obligations and age throw a woman into marriage, cutting outright any enthusiasm for education, intellectual or professional overcoming. The few who do reach it, do so thanks to their economic situation. Women, therefore, remain in a lesser valued situation in which she has to develop a future that is free from economic tutelage and has broader horizons.

INDIGENOUS WOMEN

The Peruvian population is made up of a high percentage of ethnic groups that are considered inferior, coming from the mountains and the jungles. Indigenous women are accustomed to misery and the indifference of public powers. They withstand their abandonment with philosophical resignation, yet they do not seem to lose hope for a better day. Hardworking women who are peasants, social workers, midwives, do not get adequate time off and continue to be subjected to an abnormal situation, verging on the age of feudalism or slavery. Cases still exist where girls from the mountains or the jungles are imported so that they come 'down' to the capital to serve in Lima homes or in provincial capitals, where they are subjected to inhuman treatment without any law that they know of can reach them.

A good part of this social group now makes up what we call the 'pueblos jóvenes' 'young towns' who emigrated from their own lands because geological phenomena pushed them to the cities in search of better opportunities to help them survive. Women come with their husbands, children, and even animals to invade unoccupied faraway lands and remake their precarious lives with the security that things will improve. They are all united by the same expectations and the harshness of their destiny, seemingly abandoned by the authorities. This is how they survive. In her desperate struggle to come out ahead, women's work is as self-sacrificing as men's or more.

The intelligence of these human groups is well-known. They are undaunted and show courage, and even audacity to fight for their place in the invaded areas or in the locations where they have settled in order to become temporary traders, a profession that is unknown to them in their provinces, except during the fairs when in some festivities, they offer their meager products in exchange for what they need.

And in this drama, women play a spontaneous role as worker and defender of her rights. A dark sense of survival sharpen intelligence and the impression awakened in the Lima population is well-known because of the assuredness with which she assumes her role, not of a recent arrival but a veteran of these times of crisis. This confirms the race's abilities, its sense of dignity when it is not subjugated but can behave freely, even if it is in difficult conditions of her new standard of living.

The marginal neighbourhoods, the belt of misery that surrounds Lima and that has already stretched past its limits, introducing itself into the capital city, signify an inability to withstand the overwhelming provincial misery, punished by nature's events and the authorities' laziness for not foreseeing these calamities, until they are obliged to emigrate in search of less inhumane living conditions.

These women, who have already make contact with the people of Lima, easily how much is offered to their curiosity and worries, and many of them are being instructed about matters that concern them with respect to their rights as human beings and the place that they should occupy within society.

FLORA TRISTAN'S FEMINISM

It is not just in "Women's Freedom or the Pariah's Statement" published after her death that Flora demonstrates her profound feminist calling but in all of her career as a social fighter and especially in her book "Worker's Union" in which she remarks that the cited international organization should be based on a constituency of 'male and female workers' since she never excludes women from those expressed by her nominated in whose context "should appear only those workers who do not have any property of their own, only their arms" including women workers to those whom she considers as the other half of the force involved in the WORKERS UNION.

Researching the roots of her feminism, her biographers concluded that it is found in her own marital experience, when she endured the hard condition of knowing what it is like to be a diminished being, without rights, who is ordered about and told what to do by her despotic husband and from whom she suffers humiliation, beatings, and slanderous insults. Her experience is also found in her contact with the working women of France and England, where women's work is undervalued and badly paid, and also, from her knowledge in Peru of the discriminatory treatment given to Peruvian women based on their social class, or as slaves or as objects of pleasure.

Flora says: "The most oppressed man can oppress another human being, which is his wife. Women are the female proletarians of the same male working class". And she warns that the "Declaration of the Rights of Man and the Citizen" does not include women's rights.

The laws that do not allow her to liberate herself from her husband authorize him to pursue her at any time, accuse her of being an adulteress, a tramp, a schemer, almost with impunity.

Flora emphasizes that this situation for women is due to their ignorance.

She insists in the need to awaken her intelligence with education, as one of the weapons for her liberation.

Flora proposes replacing the Divorce Law and the free choice of spouse, without influence of any kind, defending the will of the bride and groom and without the intervention of economic interests.

She reports that the Church with its discriminatory doctrine considers women as the root of all evil, the cause of original sin. Therefore, she is kept excluded from rights within the Church and is not free to divulge it openly.

With astonishing intuition for her time, Flora discovers that men and women are exploited by the same exploiters, the bosses, who consider them to be inferior to them a situation that the workers have accepted and have believed it really because of their ignorance.

"I maintain that the freedom of the workers is impossible as long as women remain in a state of stultification . . .

"I maintain that freedom for the workers is impossible as long as women remain in a suppressed state. That halts all progress" . . . and later, "Workers, try to understand this well: the law that enslaves women and denies her education also oppresses you, the proletariat men." [1]

Tristan also believed that the proletariat should organize itself as a "class", the working class. She showed how the ignorance of the working class allowed them to be fooled and confused by the bourgeoisie. They should not expect

---

[1]   Flora Tristan. "The Workers Union" "La Union Obrera" Editorial Fontamara. Barcelona: 1977

anything from the middle class as expressed by her words: "nor should you expect anything unless it comes from your own action . . . It is up to you alone to act in the interest of your own cause . . ." This announcement predated the Marxist postulate of: "The liberation of the workers will be the work of the workers themselves."

Flora petitioned: "The two requirements that should satisfy society are the recognition of: the right to work and the right to organize labour." She would never abandon this premise and remained faithful to it until the last moments of her life. In order to achieve these postulates, the first action was to unite all of the oppressed who were considered inferior, working men and women from all social classes. Said union should be recognized by Parliament where it would have a legal representative for all of the working class to monitor proceedings and demand the dictation of the laws that would meet their demands for justice. Flora watched the followers of Fourier and Owen because they never organized the working class into associations, which is the only thing that can guarantee against oppression and hunger. In union organization, the process itself lacked the strength needed to confirm her projections when she said that the working class only had its labour source, their arms, and the only guarantee of success in their struggle would be a workers union for both men and women. Tristan never ignored working women in her projections of a Workers Union since she saw them as a deciding factor in the liberation movement. [2]

In Tristan's thesis and in the roots of the Worker's Union, her most recent biographies discover the idea of a political party for representation in Parliament that lacks claims to power-driven aspirations. Definitely, the Workers Union as Tristan projected it did not have union goals like those of guilds. Tristan's idea, which is clearer today, is a Workers Political Party since the Workers Union would include the implicit—and explicit—recognition of all of the proletariat's rights by society as a whole. This political goal included global and political tasks, not simply the defense of a guild. Flora admonished the workers on existing general work conditions and warned them that they would always continue to be workers because these are the conditions that capitalism imposes on them. This previously unexpressed thesis indicated the irreversibility of the condition of the working class condition. As such, the Workers Union is the only political strategy for obtaining substantial advantages through representation before Parliament and the oppressing groups.

Flora continued to broaden her criteria on those who dictated the laws, and confirmed that property owners and

[2]   The Workers Union

the ruling class that monopolized Parliament made the laws. As long as they were in power, they would deny entry to the oppressed classes. Thus Flora realized the State's roll in defending the interests of the dominant class. Her extraordinary social and political intuition allowed her to clearly see the importance of organizing for the members of the proletariat. Without organization, the Cartists struggles for the right to a universal vote lacked strength.

Flora pledged to convince women to join the proletariat in their struggle since it was the only alternative for their complete liberation. She also pledged to convince the proletariat that without women's liberation they would never achieve their goal of emancipation.

FLORA'S INTERNATIONALISM

From the first conception, Flora regards The WORKERS UNION as an international organism and stresses her un-discriminatory points of view regarding sex, nationality, religion or working class. The one condition to join the WORKERS UNION is to be a male or female worker, be fully dependent on their work and be penniless. She realizes that the working class has a historical mission to accomplish in society. She motivates it to be aware of their power and spurs it to pursue its responsibility. She incites them: "you, workers, de-facto victims of inequity and injustice, have to establish over this earth the kingdom of justice and absolute equity between men and women". To Flora, as well as latter to Marx, the proletariat has a historical mission to attain, as it constitutes itself into a social class that carries an implicit change in the economic structure. Flora is fully conscious that the bourgeoisie's function negates the capacity to build an ideal just society. The initial task is to build the WORKERS UNION able to encourage the proletariat to its emancipation.

There is an evident coincidence between Flora's train of thought, and several years later, Marx and Engels. The writer Dominique Desanti in her book "Flora Tristan la femme Revoltee" says that it is inarguable the knowledge that Marx and Engels have of the book "Promenades dans London", where Flora describes the miserable condition that the workers class, women and children work schedules of over twelve hours, subjected to slavery regimes without working conditions security. They were fired when the employers considered it convenient, sometimes due to sickness, or any other pretext throw them out on to the street and forcing them to become beggars, or thieves without any alternative.

London, the monster city, which is the way she calls it in her third edition of the book that carries the same name, is by that time, one of the capitals with the largest delinquent population, where misery and crime go hand by hand. By the same token, the bad habits proliferated among individuals of the high class and crime is frequent in the London area.

Flora forms her experiences in her visits forced by circumstances and although she is a young woman, she is observant and shrewd, gifted with the curiosity given by the observance of the suffering of the vulnerable, who live in the suburbs and marginal neighbourhoods, where she is taken by her instinctive feeling of solidarity.

The "Promenades dans London" arouses an unusual curiosity, in London as well as in Paris, due to the denouncement contained in this book, exposing the social organism of the world's powerful, for which the poor, the beggar, the ragged, only deserved a look of repulsion or disgust.

SOME OF FLORA'S INFLUENCES

In her most recent biographies, it is told that her ideas with respect to women, and to her social problems of inequity and oppression by men, started most likely by the readings that came to her curiosity. One of them was the Irish writer Mary Wollstonecraft's book: "Women's Rights Vindication" [1] which she read in 1825, convalescent from her daughter Aline's birth. At this time the first

---

[1] Mary Wollstonecraft, A Vindication of the Rights of Woman. 1972.

discrepancies with her husband had blown up, and she had gone through her first separation.

She had already read Saint-Simon and Chateaubriand.

In her first absence from Paris, fleeing from her husband, Flora travels as the helper for a British family. She visits Switzerland, Germany, Italy, and England.

In 1829 she meets Prosper Enfantin, Saintsimonian and the Societary School. She reads the famous poet Marcela Desbordes-Valmore.

Her cultural baggage starts to grow without big pretenses. Her presence in the Parisian intellectual circles is always welcome, since her beauty and her youth crown her intelligence.

UTOPIANISM OF FLORA TRISTAN

She stoop up among the utopianisms of her time, Flora even don't identify with their postulates **even though they stirred her sensibility and found positive aspects** within them. Flora tries to interpret, analyze and study them. Her experience from the direct interaction with the workers lives, French as well as British, give her a different perspective. London, city that she visited several times and knows as well as her birthplace, give her a lesson on the brutal exploitation that the worker are victim of, disregarding their health or their most urgent needs. She learns consciously the way the women workers and their children are exploited; she discovers that when work is scarce, women suffer double discrimination, since they are either fired, or her pay will be dropped to less than half of men's, in spite of her production being the same or better. Many times they are forced into prostitution when they cannot find work in order to make ends meet.

The Utopianism ideals don't contemplate the realities the workers, men, women and children; they are submerged in. Children suffer a cruel treatment without consideration to their age, lack of strength and are forced to labour twelve hour shifts like the rest of adults.

Subsequently to her return from Peru, Flora dedicated herself to learn of the workers life and interact directly with them. She frequently visits the slums, humid basements, all inhospitable places where promiscuity reigns and contributes to destroy health and life of the weak. The masses of ignored people that proliferate and produce labour force that the bourgeoisie capitalism uses. Her children follow mother in their mass consciousness and join the labour force. Ernest becomes a mechanic labour and Aline becomes an apprentice in a women's garments factory.

Not other social fighter of the times has exerted such active proselytism with the deep knowledge of the labour class as Flora Tristan. The Utopians, Chartists, Owenists were on the fledging steps of their social ideology. They were trying to discover new realities to support their theories, but in their majority they presented idealistic schemes which were borderline with the bourgeoisie interests, which they hoped to get concessions from. They placed the ultimate solution to their problems in obtaining the "Carta Magna" to dictate or modify laws, but all of these predicates lacked any social foundation and were too far from describing the socio-economic reality. For these reason, under different categories, these groups were called Utopists. They merely defined unionism as a labour force defense, only dabbing on what Flora discovers as a redeeming method: Workers Union, the only fighting means to obtain labour security and workers emancipation.

Marx and Engels, creators of the "Historic Materialism", which would eradicate all the utopist enunciates, pointing out the pertinent actions to frame that particular epoch: Capitalism, Industrialization and birth of the Workers Class, were mere youngsters.

Among these arguments, Flora's postulates constitute an invaluable contribution, because the Workers Union contains the most emphatic social doctrine for the workers Class defense: The joining together, the universal unification of proletarians. Armed with this power, nothing will stand in the way of Justice victory, with the fundamental statement that was later stated by the "Communist Manifesto" written by Marx and Engels:

!!!**Workers of the World Unite**!!!

Flora's closest project to the utopian model, was the building of the "WORKER'S PALACES" which was compared to the agriculture communes, phalanxes, and the so called Women's Shelters. Flora adopts this system because she is aware of the neglect that the workers class is plunged in. She finds this "PALACES" as refuge for the injured or sick workers—Social Assistance—or for the derelict elders as aid in their old age. By the same token, she includes the children to keep them away from mendicancy, hunger, and stimulate education among them to acquire the knowledge that will liberate them from misery and ignorance. In the same manner, to help women workers to improve their living conditions in the same competence as men. "PALACES" would serve an enormous social influence as a refuge of security and peace to all their components, without obstructing their production within the "PALACE"s walls, encouraging productivity and cooperation.

Flora proclaims the defense and dignity of manual labour, detested by the bourgeoisie and converted in shame and derision. Manual labour rehabilitation is considered by Flora a duty and sacred right.

—0—

INITIAL STAGE OF THE PIONEER

The life and actions of Flora Tristan can be divided into two stages: before, and after her trip to Peru.

The first stage is constituted by her formation as a woman. Born in social privilege, through her first infancy she enjoyed the comfort of money, but this is followed by the direst poverty because of the negligence and abandonment from her Peruvian family. After her father's death, they stopped all financial support that Flora was entitle to because Flora, her mother, and Flora's younger brother were the only kinship of Mariano Tristan y Moscoso; therefore, heir to his abundant fortune administered by the father's younger sibling in Peru: Uncle Pio.

Victim of poverty; the first prey was her younger brother. Flora has to work as a colour technician in a lithography shop. She marries the owner one year later under her mother's pressure in an attempt to dodge indigence. This marriage ended in a stormy separation, which shaped the most painful chapter of her drama.

The second stage starts with her trip to Peru, which she makes not only to recover his father's fortunes, as many biographers agree, but she went searching for moral and social support from her relatives. She never forgot that she belonged to one of the richest families of Arequipa, from which she hoped to get understanding for her misfortunes, support, and affection.

From this trip she never got the justice that she was entitled to nor the treatment that she hoped for, but avarice and selfishness. Following the trip Flora suffers a harsh transformation of character, because she finds out the true nature of her relatives, and with that the collapse of her illusion to settle her painful poverty, recover her financial security and the tranquility of her ill-fated existence.

Flora then decides to stir her life toward other courses not thinking anymore about his father's fortunes, nor her relatives support and affection, but decides to dedicate her life, without any other purpose than the struggle of the forsaken. Back in Paris she is accosted by the husband who wants to reclaim her as his own wife, who ensues persecutions that she and her children must suffer, which forces her to roam.

Around France and goes once again back to England. In this city she contacts the Owenism and Chartism, receiving again their education and doctrine.

London still was the wicked place that she knew with its raw reality and abysmal differences that still prevail between rich and poor, between powerful and destitute.

She remembered the horror and repulsion that she felt while she stayed in Peru to the sight of hordes of native and black slaves, treated worst than beasts, and brutally mistreated for any fault that they incurred into.

In the British metropolis, Flora pried into the marginal neighbourhoods, the reeking stays; she observes the sordid way of life of workers, women, and children.

It is the visualization of this cruel and pitiless world, of which she is as well a victim, what influences this exceptionally sensitive human being to lean deeper and deeper in favor of the fight for vindication of the rights of the wretched, women, and children.

This is the birth of the Messiah Woman.

Her trip to Peru was a learning experience about her relative's true nature, and the awareness of a society that she was part of, but that she criticizes without reservations, learning the negative features of the newly emancipated

Peruvians who would have preferred to continue under the monarchy of Spain, rather than citizens of a free republic.

Her celebrated book "A Pariah's Peregrinations" was a fruit of this trip; edited in Paris in 1838. Her relatives will repudiate her for writing this manuscript, and they will burn all copies of it that they received from France as act of Faith. At the same time his uncle cuts her small allowance that he had set as a gesture of generosity, not of justice.

None of these seems to bother the pariah who has already set her path. To Flora, her only family is the disinherited, the sorrowful humanity, and her own children form part of it.

She is known first as the Pariah; then the Messiah Woman. This nickname appeared when she fully assumed her role of defender of the oppressed, which came to fit her perfectly well on her proselytizing throughout France. She stimulated the workers alliance to enable them to assume their own defense against the exploiters, and establish a social organization, as powerful as she later describes it in her book: "THE WORKER'S UNION".

Her short life, intense, and her thankless activity to serve the disinherited do not leave any room to place her within the times. She could be tied to the Utopians, the Fouriers, the Owens, the Saint—Simonians or the Constant.

Flora had reached a full understanding of the economic structures contained within the social ideas, still not defined, but she already had a luminous inspiration from them. She would have become not only a lone preacher of the workers unification but the unquestionable leader of a social movement of such pristine socialist principles with the clever conception of struggle of classes that she discovered and pointed to, and her main argument for the emancipation of women as an indispensable principle of men's liberation.

All of these arguments place Flora Tristan, taking into account the epoch, as an exceptional woman fighter, pioneer of socialism, creator of the Universal United working class and illustrious defender of Women's Rights.

FLORA TRISTAN,
FORERUNNER WOMAN

FIRST PART

CHAPTER I

THE DAUGHTER OF MARIANO TRISTAN

Flora's father, Mariano de Tristan y Moscoso (1760-1807) was an aristocrat, native of the city of Arequipa, Peru and a Peruvian Colonel of Spanish descent. He was like all privileged Spanish Americans who lived in Europe and were educated there; he left the management of their affairs with their foremen or administrators. The majority had great wealth that consisted, as in the Tristan's case in large estates with hundreds of native and black African slaves.

Our heroine's birth occurred after the events of the Napoleonic Wars and the re-establishment of the Bourbons, which resulted in French emigrations to neighbouring countries, in this case to Spain, where the noble Tristan and the beautiful Anne-Pierre Laisnay, (1772-1842) [1] also an emigrant, met by chance in Bilbao. At that time, the subjects of the King of Spain could not get married without the King's consent. Mariano was still a Spanish subject so he had to petition this formal requirement from the Crown. But, without giving it a second thought, and with the help of a Spanish priest, he chose a religious ceremony with Anne-Pierre. The marriage was never legitimized.

Flora, the Tristan—Laisnay's first daughter, was born when they returned to Paris a short time later. She was baptized in the aristocratic tradition, with the names Flora, Celestine, Therese, Henriete Tristan y Moscoso. She was born on April 7, 1803.

The Tristan—Laisnay family settled in a residential neghbourhood, as they had once in Spain, with amenities that befitted to their economic and social status. Spanish American travelers came to their house to enjoy the couple's friendship and hospitality. It is said that a young man with penetrating eyes, and nervous and energetic gestures used to attend these cultural gatherings at the Tristan—Laisnay's home. In time, he would become the

---

[1] Bacacorzo Gustavo. "Flora Tristan Personalidad Contestataria Universal". Biblioteca Nacional del Peru. Fondo Editorial. 2000. Dos volumes. Anne-Pierre, not Therese. Pag. 101 of Tomo 1.

liberator of a continent: Simón Bolívar. The future great man was able to maintain a cordial friendship with Colonel Tristan and his wife despite their political differences: Bolívar was an ardent separatist and antimonarchist, while Tristan was a loyal subject of the King of Spain.

During his frequent visits to the Tristan's home, Bolívar used to stroll through the gardens holding hands with the couple's pretty daughter while discussing with her father the serious problems that afflicted the destiny of the Americas at the time. Flora never forgot her father's relationship with Bolívar; one of her books, "Bolívar's Letters", is a collection of the letters that Bolívar exchanged with her father when she was just a young child. The letters have notes and comments by Flora.

Also, Flora used Bolívar's testimony during her trip to Peru so that her uncle Pío would investigate the friendly relationship between Bolívar and her parents in her home in Paris where everyone witnessed his appreciation and respect for the Tristan Laisnay couple, whom the uncle refuse to acknowledge. "The famous Bolívar will confirm that he was my parent's friend in Paris" she told her uncle Pío in one of her letters.

One of Flora's biographers, Ventura García Calderón, speculates on what could have been her destiny, leaving aside if both of them, courageous defenders of the rights of the oppressed, had met again and become a formidable couple, united by the same ideal of liberation and love's imperative. But when Flora traveled to Peru, Bolívar had already passed the splendours of his glory and his tragic descent was drawing near, as he was a victim of betrayals and ungratefulness despite his relentless devotion to the liberation of Spanish America.

The sudden death of Flora's father in 1807, when she was just four years old presented the family the mother and the two children, with the most precarious economic situation since they were lacking documents proving the legality of the marriage. The Peruvian ambassador aggravated the situation by collecting all of Colonel Tristan's papers. The French Government seized the couple's home because it belonged to a Spaniard and, at the time, France was at war with Spain. To cap it all, the family in Peru permanently cancelled funds for the family of the deceased in Paris. In such dire straits, the mother and her two children were forced to relocate outside Paris, where Flora and her family began the hard life that overshadowed the girl's childhood. This poverty debased Flora, her mother and her young brother who died at the age of 10 as a result of their life of misery.

Thus, Flora came to know the ghettoes of Paris where society's scum wandered, the damned and the prostitutes, who the rich and powerful push to the margins so as not to feel their presence nor know their suffering.

First as a child then as a teenager, Flora could not be indifferent later to such a radical change in her life especially since her first steps were surrounded by comfort and well-being. Nothing foretold of the sudden poverty with all of its resulting shame, repression, hunger and misery.

When she was 16 years old, Flora started to work as a colour technician in a lithography shop. She had learned to draw and absorbed the lessons that her mother gave her during their series of problems, since paying for a formal education was impossible. There are no records of Flora having learned at an institution of higher education or having chosen any other means of education. The truth is that she was really self-taught with enough audacity to become cultured and with a great ability to absorb readings. But, when she became a colour technician, she was just a worker who needed to make a living.

Given the dark situation in which they struggle, encouraged by her mother's hints the owner of the lithography shop business; married 17 years old Flora, before a year had passed. Mr. Chazal, though head-over-heels in love with this young employee, lacked the tact to deal with someone who had not forgotten her privileged early years. The differences in character between the stubborn, authoritarian husband and the proud, dignified wife, caused the first altercations that later would constantly unsettled the household peace. The births of the first two children and the decline of the printing business placed the couple in violent situations. Poverty did not disappear and the husband demanded Flora's degradation as well as all sorts of sacrifices by her to save the household finances. [1] Whereas waiting for the birth of the mismatched couple's third child, Flora decided to abandon the household and separate from her husband. But, at that time, France had suppressed the divorce law and legal separations were no longer possible. The laws drastically tied the wife to her husband's oppressive yoke. Flora, unable to endure this situation of continued violence, decided to fool her husband and tells him that she is going to her mother's house for a while outside of the city so that her children can breathe a bit of fresh air. She does just that, but with the intention of never returning to Chazal.

And so begins the period of the Pariah's persecution as she flees throughout France, stalked and followed by her husband. Flora takes her poor children from one place to

---

[1] Dominique Desanti, "Flora Tristan, la Femme Revoltée" A Woman in Revolt: a biography of Flora Tristan", Hachette. Paris: 1972. The biographer records that Chazal suggested to Flora that she become a prostitute.

another so that they cannot be snatched away by her enraged husband. She hid in the homes of friends then traveled to London, where she worked for an English family for two years.

Meanwhile, the children stayed hidden from their father under her mother's care. By this point, Flora's daughter Marie Aline had already been born; Flora sees her birth of as a comfort in her suffering. Flora starts a new life in London, where socialist movements were already taking shape under Fourier and the first utopians. She is interested in becoming part of this social environment that is more advanced than in France.

Flora visits the slums and sees the misery of this city of budding industrialism, steel, coal and textile factories where men, women and children work 12 hour shifts and where hunger, illness and misery enslave them in their poor homes.

From 1826 to 1828, Flora traveled to Switzerland, Germany, and Italy while employed by the same English family. During her travels, she always had new experiences that would affect her later on. She is already familiar with the work of author Mary Wollstonecraft "Women's Rights Vindication" and recognizes from this book a new archetypal for women.

Back in Paris, she will demand from her stubborn husband the separation of bodies and goods. The law imposed to Flora to financially support of her children and pay for all their expenses.

In 1829, her first son passes away. In the mean time she occasionally worked as a nanny, a translator and a personal assistant, among other professions. She read with passionate interest, always eager to learn and acquire more knowledge. Even though she did not have a wider choice of readings, she always managed to find something that interested her. During this time she read the famous poet Marceline Desbordes Valmore.

She met Prospero Enfantin, a Saint-Simonian and a member of the Societary School, both forerunner movements of the Utopian Socialism.

Flora met an official of the merchant navy called Zacharias Chabrié and sends with him a first letter to her uncle Pío, who resided in Peru. In this letter she confided her situation. Her uncle replied to this letter in October of 1830.

Affected by the revolutionary ideas of the time, she participated with the people of London in the 1830 manifestations, which were generated by the overthrown of Charles X and the transformation of Louis Philippe in "the King of the French", not "of France". Flora witnessed other meetings of the London workers, but no movement like the previously mentioned had so powerfully impressed her.

In the meantime, her husband did not stop persecuting her, demanding his children back. Flora was attacked and hurt in the street. She found herself obliged to give her son back to her husband, but she kept her daughter.

Flora discovered that during her absence Chazal had abandoned the workshop, and overwhelmed by his debts he had turned to alcoholism. She had already sent to the Parliament her request to reconsider the law of divorce, which was discussed and finally approved in 1884 (forty years after her death). The idea of being enslaved to Chazal fills her with anguish and despair and so she tries to avoid him, which makes her feel like escaping delinquent, and such idea, persistently worries her.

Out of necessity, Flora had started to write commentaries for newspapers. This helped her to provide for her needs and those of her daughter. At the same time, she wrote about the problems that she herself endures due to the situation that she was subjected to by the laws that merely dealt with women's problems. These were her first acts of rebellion against the injustices of which she was a victim herself.

Flora longed to communicate, to express her ideas as well as her understanding of the events that had occurred in Paris, with their changes and repercussions. She was aware of the trial of (Barthelemy-Prosper) P. Enfantin and other socialists and was affected when she found out that they had been condemned to a year in prison for their ideas. The Saint-Simonians had just tried to publish a weekly entitled: "The Liberated Woman" but their attempt was cut short by persecution.

Her uncle Pío wrote to her again this time invited her to travel to Peru but without giving an explanation.

Flora decided to travel to Peru. This opened the door to the hope of recovering her father's fortune and leaving behind the long battle against poverty. Yes, she knew that this was going to be the adventure of her life.

In 1833, she traveled to Bordeaux where she contacted one of her father's distant relatives, Mariano Goyeneche, who organized her trip to Peru. In the first phase, she bonded with those who could advise her and facilitate her trip. She had brought her little daughter with her, and left her in the care of a good woman, the landlady of the boarding house where she spent her days before the trip. In Bordeaux, Flora again met the sailor Zacharias Chabrié, who was now the captain of the boat called the "Mexican" that she would travel in. Flora experienced more than a few problems while trying to hide her status as a married woman with children. The Peruvians from the consulate recognized Flora as the daughter of Mariano Tristan because of her strong resemblance to him. Nobody was surprise by her trip, despite the many difficulties that presented themselves but which they helped her with. Commander Chabrié was flattered by the presence of the young niece of a famous Peruvian, with whom he had a friendship. When the preparations were finished, Flora ensured her daughter Aline's stay at the boarding house under the landlady's care, who assures her that she would care for Aline until Flora returned. If Flora did not return, the landlady promised to be a mother to Aline.

The day Flora turned thirty years old, April 7th 1833; she embarked the "Mexican" to go to her father's motherland.

Due to the unbearable situation with her husband, Flora hid her marriage and children from her Peruvian family. She did not know what they would think about her because they never replied to the letters her mother had sent to her uncle Pío for more than 20 years. She was very cautious about the information she disclosed to her uncle, because she was aware of the prejudices of her aristocratic Peruvian family. However, her mother always reminder her about her father's message before dying: "you have Pío left, you have Pío left". Neither her mother nor she forgot this unattainable resource. This time the uncle Pío himself invited her to Peru, and she was hopeful to receive her father's inheritance. The journey was so long! Her heart beat with excitement to the idea of meeting her famous uncle Pío.

Unfortunately, Flora naively made a big mistake that was hard to take back. In her last letter to her uncle, she decided to be honest and share with him her mother's situation. Her mother's marriage could not be legalized in France, so it only remained valid religiously. Thus, the laws of the time indicated that she was an illegitimate daughter. However, when her father was alive their friends always respected the Tristan family and no one ever questioned the legitimacy of their marriage.

When Flora went on board she realized that she was the only woman travelling with twenty men for four long months out in the sea. But the respectful friendship with Commander Chabrié cheers her up and she feels confident of the journey been the favourite traveler. Deep down, she senses that she will enter a period of solitude and will be at the mercy of her own thoughts. She started a travel journal, which would later become the memoirs that will have the name of "Peregrinations of the Pariah", a book that would be edited in Paris.

An event of great repercussion takes place in Lyon during Flora journey. A strike movement is generated by the silk weavers with extraordinary transcendence. At her return, Flora will have knowledge of this fact and will investigate in detail, as part of her experiences fighting for the working class.

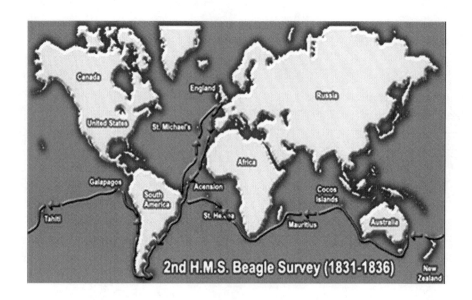

MAP
OF THE TRIPS

CHAPTER II

PERU: LONGING AND FRUSTRATION

The detailed story of Flora Tristan's journey to Peru is told over 400 pages in the two volumes of her book "Peregrinations of a Pariah", which was published in Paris three years after she returned to Paris. Flora used to keep a journal of her life; at she did so when she boarded the 'Mexican'. But her book contains much more than her diary. The Introduction explains the reasons behind the book, and includes remarks about her family. Although in the Dedication to the Peruvians, she refers to them as her friends and countrymen. [1]

---

[1] "Dedication to the Peruvians . . . Having proved it, I have said that the upper class in Peru is profoundly corrupt and that its egoism leads it to anti-social attempts at satisfying their desire for luxury, their love of power and their other passions" Flora Tristan. "Perégrinations d' une paria—A pariah's journey. Paris: 1838

The trip was about 5 months long and, as the only woman aboard she must have produced a natural interest from the 20 other passengers, who were all men. Nevertheless, except for the trip's inevitable incidents of seasickness and bad weather, Flora did not write about any other inconveniences that might have made her unhappy. One of her pastimes was writing diligent notes on the trip's incidents, the disembarking in ports of call and her observations on the people that she encountered on her long journey.

At that time, trips to South America were made through the Strait of Magellan. Flora saw the entire southern coast with its flaming torches lit by locals, which is the reason why the area is known as Tierra del Fuego.

When they arrived at the bay of Praya on the African coast, Flora had the opportunity to witness the slave trade. This despicable business was carried out by foreigners, many of whom were French.

Flora feels a tremendous rejection, and notes it in her memoirs; she also shares it with her countrymen, occasional guests in her ports of call. The South American countries had already proclaimed their independence, but it did not affect the slaves for several years to come.

Her arrival to the Peruvian coast was filled with incidents, some were colorful, but most of them showed the state of the abandonment state of the ports, the discomfort, the lack of hygiene, and the nature of the population. Many of the inhabitants were foreign citizens who have come to Peru as fortune seekers, with veiled political and personal motives, with countless delinquents among them. Some of the newcomers came to the far South American beaches by fate and they have made a home at the new places, always feeling nostalgic, and never leaving behind their homeland. It seemed as if they were all forced by adversity, but they all aimed to amass big fortune, and go back to their homeland to enjoy it. Foreign men and women that approached Flora, while she was in Peru, did so to complain, to scorn, and ridicule the natives, racially mixed and criollos; although, many of them defeated by circumstances, had built families, and adjoined the Peruvian society. A case in point was Althaus, a professional German military, who would service a country at random only to satisfy his need to exercise his skills. Althaus come to Peru seeking to remind in battle, after serving in Germany and France; he married a relative of the Tristan's family, becoming Flora's distant cousin.

Althaus took part in the post-independence Peruvian military turmoil, leading uprisings to get a hold of the political power.

The Peruvian's ignorance of war techniques gave way to the most unexpected victories in the continuous local subversive movements. Flora received reports of all these particulars, making lively commentaries about them with her distant cousin. Flora continues writing in her diary pages every detail of her stay in Peru as a habit of her spirit of observation, and as her natural resentment against her Peruvian relatives, which she never seduced as family, and was never accepted as such. This anomaly kept her from breaking the chain of intolerable misfortunes, calamities, misery and disillusionment of her life in Paris. Flora wanted to be loved by the ones she considered her close relatives, the brother, cousins, his father's nephews. She wanted to belong to the country's social environment that she thought was hers, and on which she placed all her expectations, including admitting her legal marital status, her children, her mother. She planned to bring them all to Peru creating this way a new home.

Flora's dreams projected as far as possibly acting in the political and social arena of this country. Flora focused all her European knowledge in order to better the condition of the Peruvian people. She considered them naturally intelligent and deserving of better living, if it was not for the ruling system of slavery which they were submerged in. It was also due to the ignorance of men and women, whose lives were lodged in leisure and the delights of fortune, unless they fell from grace, like her cousin Carmen whose well-being, depended upon uncle Pio's kindness. The black slaves lived a vile existence in the large haciendas of the country.

Flora's stay in her father's country, Arequipa, was a succession of learning experiences about human nature, greed and selfishness of the rich; owners of so many riches were incapable of an effort to alleviate the suffering of their fellow men. Not even the call of their own blood to make justice to the ones that deserve it. In Peru as well as in Europe, despot laws tied the freedom of the weak. In this country, women who did not want to tie their live in the matrimonial institution had to confine themselves to a convent. Flora was as well tied to her odious husband, but soon her day of total liberation would come.

Lengthy was her seven months of residence in Arequipa. Her thoughts were always on her children, whom she could not get any news from. She had to endure her uncle Pio's odd behavior, whom she only met several months after he arrived from the hacienda, even though he was aware of her arrival. He seemed to be too busy with the financial preoccupations, or did not have any interest to see his niece. The day that she could finally embrace him in a hug, a profound happiness filled her up, because she was in the arms of her father's brother. She had waited so long for this moment, but very big was her disappointment when both, uncle and niece, faced the issue about the niece's rights. After long circumlocutions and lacking the courage to face her uncle, she had the terrible shock to hear him say that since she was the illegitimate daughter of his brother Mariano, she had no rights to the inheritance. She reasoned in vain the arguments contained the circumstances of her parents' marriage, and sudden death of her father, without having the chance to legalize the wedding; nonetheless, all her arguments were insufficient for uncle Pio to admit her as the legitimate daughter born in such dire circumstances. This was reiterated by the laws of Spain as well as the ones ruled in Peru.

Based on uncle's Pio generosity, he assigned her an allowance in Paris, and the return fare.

Frustrated her hope Flora decided to return to Paris, stopping in Lima for two months visiting uncle Pio's relatives.

Lima as well as Arequipa surprised her by its luxury, women's frivolity, and disdain for culture. Women had invented a curious costume, petticoat long skirt and shawl, which maintained their anonymity while satisfying all their whims, allowing them to cover their faces but for one eye.

Flora noticed that the Lima women exercised a real influence in the political and social life without inhibitions of any kind, with acute intelligence; their only setback would be their lack of culture, except in music, dance and domestic arts. Similar to her reflections about Arequipa, she made a variety of commentaries to the disapproval of Peruvians since in the prologue of the historian Jorge Basadre. He criticizes her for her excessive censorship of the Peruvians, based specially in their flaws generated as a consequence of independence war and divergences between the military leaders.

Arequipa became a tension center with repercussions in the capital, created by the Spanish heritage and its ever present aristocracy, many of whom yearned for the colonial system, with its titles and privileges. Besides the fact that inhabitants could not admit that the liberators were not Peruvians, but imported armies and that the honor of independence laid on Colombians, Venezuelans, and even Chileans. Offensive phrases tumbled around, saying that: "Peru had been liberated from colonialism by foreigners." Peruvians disregarded as well, perhaps rancorously, the Túpac Amaru revolution from merely 40 years before,

La tapada limeña

which stirred up the whole South American continent, arousing thousands of indigenous natives that paid with their lives the gesture of liberation against the brutal Spanish oppression, becoming this way the precursors of American Liberation in 1780.

In Lima, Flora meets a woman, besides politicians, militaries, aristocrats, and descendants of the colony in process of adaptation. This woman is the only one that awakes her admiration and piety: the famous Francisca Zubiaga de Gamarra, nicknamed la Mariscala [1]. Even though she is in the sunset of her glory, and the same age as Flora, she is armed with the courage and intelligence that women are capable when they find the suitable field to develop their innate qualities and controlling over the incapable masses. These kinds of women take initiative by themselves and grab the responsibility demanded by the circumstances to maintain the political power in an ungovernable country eaten away by anarchy, and besieged by the greed of the ones that pretend its domination as

---

[1] Francisca Zubiaga de Gamarra took active part in Peru's struggles for independence as did many other women in Peru. When the Liberator Simon Bolivar arrived in Cuzco, the city offered him a tribute by presenting him with a gold and diamond crown of laurels. It was the young Mrs. Gamarra who placed it on the Liberator's head but he, knowing how this lady had contributed to the struggle for Peru's liberty, gave the crown back to her by placing it on her head in sincere homage.

their exclusive right. That was the history of the newly emancipated America, and the situation faced by la Mariscala, the Peruvian first lady. She was the Mariscal wife, who governs Peru between 1829-33, 1838-40, and 1840-41. The lucky leaders grab and handover the political power in this way.

La Mariscala made a profound impression in Flora's sensibility even more when she heard her brief but courageous story. Not all was frivolity in Lima. La Mariscala was an example, good or bad, of the intelligence and shrewdness of a woman.

Flora obtained an interview with la Mariscala aboard the ship that took la Mariscala to her exile and death. They sympathized and la Mariscala increase her affective demonstrations to Flora because she found her a courageous woman, defender of her rights denied by her aristocratic relatives.

Flora's stay in Peru—Arequipa and Lima—leaves a deep footprint in her spirit which will guide her future actions when she is back in Paris, and undoubtedly for the rest of her life.

Flora dislikes Lima more than Arequipa; she finds it difficult to cohabit with their inhabitants. Peruvian customs are more liberal, but as well, they are indifferent to human solidarity. Distance between rich and poor are abysmal. At the capital of this brand new republic the hideous slavery system prevails. In the haciendas as well as in the domestic service of the large families, owners of large palaces, the indigenous and the black are still enslaved. Independence has no reach the lower levels of a society based on exploitation of the disinherited. Everything continues as before in the colonial regime, where the skin color, fortune, and ostentatious last names were what mark the difference. [1]

In the eve of Flora's return trip to Paris she makes a recount of her time spent and the events that she had to undergo. Flora met with her Peruvian relatives, and their customs, as well as their display of religious devotion, which is so alien to the true Christian precepts. Even in the convents they exhibit luxury and squandering. Furthermore, uncle Pío's incredible attitude which truncated her confidence, and denied all her rights to her father's inheritance. Her suffering in Peru, perhaps deeper than in Paris, the injustices, the offenses suffered from

---

[1] Flora witnessed in one of the great haciendas in Lima the cruel treatment that the pregnant women slaves were given. If they had an abortion, or refused to become pregnant, they would be punished. A pair of young women chained by their hands to a wall, fed bread and water, paid for their crime in this manner, until they be remorseful for their audacity.

her Peruvian relatives, they all pile up in Flora's heart. It is a bitter ferment that is growing in her soul because of the frustration through the best years of her life. The separation from her children, forced her to hide them for fear to scandal; the persecution and hounding threats from the husband that undoubtedly will be expecting her return.

Flora is reading Goethe's Werther, and her spirit goes through a tremendous depression. She is about to commit suicide, but she retracted because she was too young; she should overcome her suffering, and return to the struggle.

She recognizes the dawn of new longings, not to obtain material comforts from her family, but she decides to revive her battle in Paris. This time she will not be alone. She will look for the company of the disinherited, the humiliated, and the class she belongs to: the people. She has to recover her children to guide them to new feelings of human solidarity.

She should continue defined the unjust laws that have denied her of all right to life and freedom. She cannot give up because there are thousands of offended human beings insulted, to whom she must contribute to give them back their self-confidence, teach them to fight and liberate themselves from their chains of misery.

When Flora left Peru without resentments, on board of the ship that will take her back to the country of her origin, she will exclaim with profound conviction:

"From this point forward, my homeland will be humanity!"

The Woman Messiah is born.

CHAPTER III

IN PARIS AGAIN

Flora returned to Paris, the only city in the world where she enjoyed living. Her loved ones were in Paris: her children; her mother; and her friends. It was 1835, two years after her departure, and her heart was full of hope. She returned to the painful condition of an unprotected, stalked woman with a heart full of conflicting emotions and she still had no fixed goal. But no, there was a goal. She would join the battle to conquer injustice. She knew well what awaited her: a husband with an obsessive passion. Chazal had not given up trying to get his children back. Nothing could stop him. Flora was still his lawfully wedded wife and he had rights over the children. Flora's mother told her about Chazal's aggressive actions and behavior, which were increasing since he thought that Flora had regained her father's fortune. The unending battle to finally liberate her from this evil man was reborn. Flora rejoined her daughter Aline in Bordeaux. Aline had been left in the care of the generous landlady who had watched over her since Flora left for Peru.

Paris was in the period of Romanticism, the heyday of the famous George Sand. She assumed masculine identity using men's clothing, a cane and a hat, yet she concealed her real name: Aurora Dupin. Flora did not like this behavior and she showed it. George Sand put her liberal lifestyle on display without hiding her sexual relationships with various superior musicians of her time, including Chopin. Sand represented the liberated woman. As an author in the literary world, she was allowed to behave as she pleased. This was a time of liberalism in both life and thought.

Nevertheless, despite their differences, George Sand provided contributions towards the publishing of "The Worker's Union", which Flora requested from all of her friends.

Flora returned to her activities and her friends. She wrote articles in newspapers and magazines so that she could feed her daughter and herself as well. Ernest was with his father, Chazal, who continued to stalk Flora. He tried to kidnap their daughter, Aline, and at one point was successful but Flora got her back. Chazal would hurl insults at Flora and attacked her in the street. Finally, while determining the custody of the daughter during the separation process, Chazal kidnapped Aline again. His excessive behavior reached such a point that Aline escaped from the house where he held her and returned to her mother's house. Chazal sent the police to get her back. His pursuit of the possession of his two children became more and more demanding, as did Flora's desire to keep her daughter.

During this year, Flora met Fourier, the social reformer and founder of Fourierism. Fourier initiated the construction of community organizations to serve the working class. Flora gave him her essay entitled: *"Of the need to treat foreign women well"*, which refers to the mistreatment that she received from her family in Peru, which would be called: "The Peregrinations of a Pariah", in which Flora was the Pariah.

The difficult months following her return to Paris included arguments and stalking as well as contact with her friends. Aline went from her mother's care to her father since the law was strong and she had to pass into her father's hands.

Flora met Victor Considerant, one of Fourier's disciples and the group's most important leader. She increases her studies on the ideas of socialist utopianism, especially after meeting Robert Owen [1] during his visit to Paris. At the same time, Flora met the famous, edge poet, Marceline Desbordes-Valmore. In January 1837, Flora received a letter from her daughter that upset and mobilized her. Aline, barely 12 years old, wrote that she feared her father and insinuated that he had tried to abuse her. Taking advantage of a moment when no one was watching, Aline fled to her mother's house. Flora reported Chazal to the police. He was found guilty and condemned to two months in jail. The spiteful husband then accused his wife of being a tramp, an adulteress and a schemer.

Flora gained more friends in the Fourier circle. That same year, she delivered her brief treatise: "Petition to Re-establish Divorce" to the chamber of deputies. The legal ruling on their separation was not given until February, 1838. But Chazal regained his freedom and continued to harass her with his relentless pursuit. Armed with a gun, he shot her at close range and seriously wounded her. The scandal fueled expectations and interest. When Flora recovered, she wrote a: "Petition to Abolish the Death Sentence" and delivered it to the more liberal deputies. She immediately published articles in magazines and renewed

---

[1] Robert Owen, the English Reformer created the cooperative movement.

her activities. Chazal was in prison and would be tried for attempted murder. Flora published: "Peregrinations of a Pariah" immediately followed by: "Mephis or the Proletariat". Both were well received because of the events of her life. "Peregrinations of a Pariah, two volumes, 1838, were published three times. Flora achieved a few months of freedom and economic peace. Chazal would not pursue her again.

The Pariah was no longer an unknown in the Chartist world. Flora secretly traveled to London to attend a private convention by the promoters of the Magna Carta, whose leader was William Lovett. Flora continued to accumulate experiences. She visited factories, working neighbourhoods, the cesspools where the workers, their wives and children rotted, the victims of exploitation and misery. Flora was already familiar with the birthplace of industrialism, where 20 million workers were subjected to the tyranny of the more powerful who exploited their physical labour in oppressive and unfair conditions. Women were forced to work in inferior situations, replacing their husbands and often children replaced their mothers, thereby diminishing their miserable salaries, depending on the wishes of the business owners.

In London, Flora attended a session of Parliament disguised as a man. She met O'Connell [1] and O'Connor, both leaders of the Chartist movement. Flora joined the workers, researched them, and learned about their sacrifices and helplessness. No one like Flora would have greater contact with the working class, whose suffering she shared. They called her "the communist" or "the socialist" but she was received by her friends with respect and admiration. She now had a place in the fight for social justice.

Flora was strongly attracted to London. In 1840, she published "Promenades dans Londres", which had three publications, and was judged admirably by its critics. It was seen as a testimony of the inhuman situation that England's working class lived under. Flora later produced an abstract of the same book for publication in a popular edition entitled: "The Monster City".

In 1839, Chazal was condemned to 20 years of hard labour and Flora was liberated from her stalker. At the same time, parliament allowed that her children Ernest and Aline would no longer carry the surname of their father. Both children would now sign with her surname: Tristan.

---

[1] Daniel O'Connell was the salaried defender of the Irish separatists. They paid him a salary so that he could defend them before the English parliament. He is also a social activist belonging to the Cartist movement.

Flora identified herself deeply with the working class and spoke on their behalf. Her two children adopted the same profession as manual labourers. Ernest was a mechanic and enlisted in the marines. Aline was an apprentice seamstress in a workshop [2]

Flora's trips and many expenses gave her new economic worries. Her health was precarious and she spent many days trying to overcome her weakness. When she recovered, she would continue her activities, connections and publications in literary magazines.

Flora met and connected with the most famous intellectuals of her time: Lamartine, Víctor Hugo, Teófilo Gautier and others. She invited to her house those who shared her ideas, which were part of the stormy and non-conformist times they were living in.

Flora was possessed by a whirlwind of action. She was seen at all political meetings, where they discussed themes related to the formation of a new society based on the principles of utopian socialism, phalansteries, co-operativism and a decrease in working hours.

From her trips to London, Flora had knowledge of the Chartist movement and the activities of socialist groups

---

[2] Aline, Flora's daughter, married to Clovis Gauguin will later become the mother of the famous French painter, Paul Gauguin

proposing the most radical means to obtain social laws in the workers' favour. But their ideas were still vague, inconsistent and without a plan for immediate action that didn't have to wait through the long legal process for enforcement. Chartism was not able to deal with the immediate needs of the proletariat, whose state of misery was highlighted by desperation. From what she observed in London, Flora focused on the ideas of the phalansteries and their Workers Palaces, where the proletariat had the right to recovered from their sufferings and were able to acquire new knowledge that allowed them to gain better working conditions.

The Workers Palaces would become a place where the eldest workers could rest, with hospitals for the wounded, social environments for the members themselves and schools for their children and teenagers. This was a visionary project in social security for those who gave the most to society. In this way, when they suffered accidents or sicknesses, or a lack of support, they would have the necessary defenses. Most importantly, Worker's Palaces would be schools for the youngest, to eradicate ignorance, which for Flora was the source of all evil and the reason for the exploitation that the working class, men and women, were victims of.

These were the Pariah's dreams. She had already taken on her role as a fighter for social justice and she prepared for it in order to perform conscientiously.

Paris XIX century

CHAPTER IV

THE PARIAH'S MISSION

Liberated from her husband's persecution and no longer worried about her children's safety, Flora dedicates herself to her projects and to serving the social ideals in which she finds herself immersed.

She is conscious of the unjust situation for women who society does not defend but who are instead, as indicated by law and custom, grouped as inferior beings. She thinks about organizing a society or social group that defends women without families as well as honest foreign women who could join "Homes for Women" with the only obligation being to maintain dignified behavior. She also conceives her book "Woman's Emancipation" that her publisher would later, after her death, subtitle as "The Pariah's Testament". She was already published her book about Peru: "The Need to Treat Foreign Women Better"

(1835), which really contains her complaint of the unequal treatment that she suffered in her father's homeland.

She also publishes her romantic novel, "Mephis", which is her own story and the difficulties that she suffered so cruelly during her lifetime.

She prepares her book "Promenade dans Londres" that was not published until 1840-42. But it is decided to publish the Memoirs of her voyage to Peru before that. "PARIAH'S PEREGRINATIONS" regarding her stay in Peru from 1833-34 is published in two dense volumes in 1838. This book causes a real impact and it is judged to be the most courageous allegation against her Peruvian family who condemned and accused her. [1] Years later, the Peruvian historian Jorge Basadre considers it to be a magnificent literary work of unquestionable worth. [2]

With her memoirs in the form of a novel, Flora, the writer, is also creating a new genre that is not used yet and is of obvious literary quality. Her "Peregrinations . . ."

---

[1] Flora includes a terrible letter to her uncle Pio where she discovers her father's cowardly deception regarding the question of marriage.

[2] Jorge Basadre, prologue to "Peregrinaciones de una Paria". Editorial Cultura Antártica S.A." Lima 1946. Translation by illustrious Peruvian Emilia Romero in 1946 to the Universidad Nacional Mayor de San Marcos.

Capture many aspects of the recently liberated Peruvian society and life, their traditions and customs unknown in Europe, and that make up unpublished statements that are worthy of being reflected in a literary work.

The success is real and the book "Pariah's Peregrinations" has three immediate publications.

Flora dedicates her book to the Peruvians. In her dedication, which is very considerate and sincere, she signs off as: "Your friend and compatriot". In its context she does not shy away from criticizing the Peruvian society's behavior, or lack of. She categorizes it as egotistical and corrupt, with an insatiable desire for profit. She exhorts them to improve their comportment and to procure public education, especially for women whom she considers intelligent rather than frivolous and extravagant.

The reaction of her relatives in Peru is immediate. Her uncle Pío suppressed the small allowance that he assigned her. Bishop Goyeneche, her famous relative, orders the burning of the copies of her books in the Plaza in Arequipa, in an "act of faith" the same way heretics had been burned in the past.

All of which only confirmed the backward social and intellectual condition that the country is in. This society was incapable of recognizing the truth contained in Flora's book, which was turned into a novel, and then converted into a document.

Flora must have felt compensated for their humiliations and contempt, for the lack of understanding from her relatives to whom she felt obliged to advise fairly in the spirit of tolerance.

After returning from Peru, Flora identifies more and more with the working class. It is possible that she is attracted to them because of her experience during her childhood and adolescent years. She had known the most oppressive misery then, which was barely hidden in a world without compassion, a world where prostitution was the main resource for women trying to get hold of the money needed to survive. There is no proof that the girl did that and presumably that was the reason the mother advised her to accept the suitor that proposed to her, when she was only seventeen years old; she gave her consent. Not much is known about her mother before or after the father's death. The mother must have educated her with knowledge of her prior social condition, as the daughter of an American persona, and she must have had a high and conscious education, to acquire signs of higher culture than the popular society that she had to mix with during the years of her harshest indigence. She studied drawing, apparently with her mother, and acquired the habit of reading, developing her love for good customs. The mother, nor the daughter never forgot their origin, their own class, closer to the bourgeoisie that the masses, without it stopping Flora from learning and appreciated the situation of the destitute and homeless, because she was from the same social condition. Her meager education was a combination of her own spontaneous intelligence, which she showed since little, and her mother's teachings. Her mother must have come from a high class family. This fact would explained that she emigrated to Spain and came close to the high class circle where she met her future husband, and also a lot of other important persons in Spain as well as back in France. [1]

There are a lot of letters, to Flora's mother and her own that she makes mention in her memoirs, the "Bolivar Letters", which demonstrate that Anne—Pierre Laisnay was a woman from a petit-bourgeois class, not a simple woman from the street. It is possible that she could have had a superior education, which she kept throughout her life and passed to Flora, since her son died at a young age.

---

[1] The suspicion exists that Mariano Tristan had no intention of legitimizing his marriage, and that it was all a trick by the Peruvian military and lawyer. Given the fact that in the five years they lived together, he did not complete his duty or leave his wife a will.

Flora's biographers affirm that her writing had orthographic errors, major sin to the language purists, not to the ones that are urged to communicate, and in those times superior education was not accessible to women.

I bring forth the Peruvian edition of "Pariah's Peregrinations" which does not have any orthographic errors, nor semantic, or errors of composition, which would have been picked up by her Peruvian biographer, who was not too addict to the book itself and he criticizes as excessive. "Peregrinations" is a large work and there is not news that it was corrected by any language expert in the language.

On the other hand, in Flora's book "The Workers Union" published by Fontamara, in Barcelona, we do notice the hurried editing in copies of the book in the use of repetitions and grandiose expressions of the period. This is specifically due to Flora's desire to complete *her mission* and improve an understanding of the working class as if she knows that her time is short. Nevertheless, in her writing you can see the knowledge she has and the good use that she makes of it.

Among her talents, it is said that Flora was a translator. She probably translated into English since that is the country she visited the most. Before her trip to Peru, Flora had visited almost all of Europe when necessity had forced her to work as a nanny or travelling companion. It must have been easy for her to be a translator especially since she traveled to London a lot and must have spoken with male and female workers, and people like O'Connor, etc. Likewise, Flora's mother probably spoke Spanish fluently since she chose to immigrate to Spain before Flora was born. Flora must have ended up learning the Spanish that she heard as a child since, despite the many French citizens in Arequipa and Lima. She lived for almost a year among Spanish—speaking people with whom she carried on conversations without the need for a translator.

Flora's trip to Peru demonstrated her determination and intelligence as she was not intimidated by the dangers of the voyage that, at the time, was considered to be an ordeal. Especially since she was travelling in a state of personal insecurity and uncertainty, as she left her children behind exposed to their father's whims and her daughter in the care of someone she just recently met.

As described in her book "Pariah's Peregrinations" those who surrounded Flora in Peru discovered her intelligence, courage and knowledge, which was much more advanced than that of the Peruvians. Despite her uncle Pío's attitude, Flora was esteemed and valued by Peru's upper class since most of them thought that Pío was unfair.

During her stay in Peru, Flora was visited by politicians, military and society ladies who tried to acquire from uncle Pío's niece her vast knowledge of France's superior culture, the European country that she came from.

"Peregrinations . . . is a true autobiographical novel, outlining many of Flora's character traits, as well as her observational and analytical skills, which are difficult to find in an illiterate.

Flora wrote her "Promenade dans Londres" in 1840. It was so successful that two more editions were immediately published. It made an impact on readers who were interested in the topic discussed. According to critics, it was a horrific mirror of the situation and the misery of the working class who were brutally exploited by the owners of factories. The iron and charcoal metropolis installed textile machines that reduced the work by labourers, both women and men, which through them into even greater misery.

In this book, Flora reveals the state of degradation that women had reached with the increase in prostitution due to the hunger that pushes her and the begging hiding in the slums where the people live.

Her literary success is not due solely to the originality of her topic but also to the accusations contained therein, which the Pariah puts forward without adornment.

Later, Flora published portions of "Promenade dans Londres" in a popular edition called "The Monster City", which was also very successful in bookstores.

Flora did not travel to London for pleasure or because the city attracted her; she went there specifically to sink deeper, get more details on the situation of the working class. She did so in a way that no other utopian of the period would ever do it.

Deepening her thinking, she reveals that women are industry's reserve army given the lower salaries that they receive when they replace men at work.

Flora is firm in her defense of women as being exploited even more than men. She insists showing the workers that *"the liberation of the workers is impossible as long as women remain in this state of stultification. They halt all progress"*. Flora recognizes women's conservative idiosyncrasy in understanding the worker's struggles so she advises them that the businessmen who exploit the working class also oppress women. Since they are often reminded of their 'inferiority,' the oppressed begin to believe it and offer little resistance.

Flora points out the offensive meaning behind considering the women an object of sexual pleasure or a simple children producer. In addition she is also considered an exclusive housekeeper which in the working field the woman must add to these tasks helping the maintenance of the common home throughout a paid job.

Flora reclaims with her demands the intention that women obtain the following rights:

1. The right to equality in education and professional training, to gain economic independence from men and receive the same pay for the same work.
2. Right to free choice of husband, without any type of interference.
3. Right to divorce and of partner free election.
4. Right to legal support of single mothers and rights of illegitimate children part of the paternal heritance.

She restates, with the intention of influencing the working class: "Workers, try to comprehend this well: the law that enslaves women and stops them from getting education, oppresses you too, proletariat men". By her own accord, Flora intuited that her preaching did not congeal among women. She captured the attention, and is accepted by men, but women of all social classes, avoid the Pariah's teachings, and come to the point that refuse to listen to her. Flora's warnings materialize about the resulting harm from keeping women in such absolute ignorance. This is the reason she demands from the working class to include women in their union postulates, incorporating rights and obligations, this way they will get used to be part of the struggle started by men. Apart from women, Flora is listened to, admired, and perhaps loved by the men that understood, and encouraged her. She is part of the first societarios, fourierism, chartism, compagnones, and the utopist socialism. But she surpass them all, because she adds the need for the universal unity of the working class, which is the same as the Workers International, but without distinction of sex which is what makes it more original, more revolutionary.

Londres XIX century

CHAPTER V

FLORA'S POLITICAL INTUITION

Flora defines the working class as the most oppressed and miserable as well as the largest and the most necessary. This results from her observations and her own experience, having lived amongst them for the last ten years of her life. She explains that the root of the problems oppressing the proletariat is poverty. She takes the reader back to the path that leads to the formation of the oppressive class, the bourgeoisie, who had gained power through the revolution of 1789, thanks to the help of the proletariat who served as their springboard without any of the revolution's benefits. For Flora, the French Revolution is the bourgeoisie's revolution that thus erased the remains of feudalism. The proletariat could not able to understand the mechanisms of the movement created by the "third state" at the service of the emerging bourgeoisie.

Flora concludes with a categorical statement: "You cannot expect anything from the bourgeois class, don't expect them to claim or write about human rights" . . . and sentencing . . . "It is up to you alone to act in the interest of your own cause".

She then states that the two demands that should satisfied a society like this are: **recognizing the right to work and the right to organize labou**r. [1]

In order to achieve these objectives, Flora proposes the union of all of the oppressed workers and women, of all social classes in a universal association whose definition is specifically detailed in her book "THE WORKER'S UNION".

Far from economic materialism, which did not exist yet, Flora states that the industries and factory owners live at the expense of the worker with whom they attain the concept of PLUS VALIA, which is the appropriation of that which belongs to the worker without defining or clarifying the means that they use to rob the workers' rights.

In her statement on the need to organize in the WORKER'S UNION, Flora concludes: "the Worker's Union will gather together the workers, their only property being the strength of their hands".

---

[1]   This is Saint-Simon's hypothesis.

Flora discovers the concept of **social class** and states that as the **bourgeoisie** became its own class, the workers should become **a working class,** in opposition to the bourgeoisie.

When she demands the need for a paid defense to represent them in Parliament she is defining the workers' union as a political party or movement that demands the rights of the oppressed class before the public powers of Parliament. She advises that this representative should enjoy a decent salary so that he can pay for his needs as well as working costs such as the advertising needed to make known the existence of the Worker's Union to all of those who might be interested. Flora discovers the power of propaganda as an efficient means of discussion their aims. Flora had met O'Connell, the defender of the Irish cause, ". . . a man who really love the worker's. He is very loyal, legal, and in complete conformity with the rules establish by a healthy morality. His position will be rather exceptional".

None of these statements refers to guilds or trade unions. They are political and of a high unitary concept and unifying, capable of creating an indestructible force. Flora's only objective is the recognition of all of the proletariat's rights.

Yolanda Marco, who conducts research on Tristan, says of "THE WORKER'S UNION", "She does not try to segregate the oppressed groups to integrate them into an oasis of justice. Instead she considers the existing general conditions of production to be irreversible. Therefore, she is appealing to the workers who work and will continue to work under the conditions imposed upon them by capitalism. Although Flora does not go any further, the qualitative leap with regards to the Utopians is obvious"

In this way, Flora's ideas are obviously political since it is the Union that takes action in Parliament to obtain worker's rights through the proceedings of the Worker's Union representative, who will watch over and demand the passing of laws requested by them.

Flora compares the existence of the oppressed classes in all of the countries that she has visited: the slaves in Peru are the same as the workers in London or in France. She therefore insists on the idea that the working class has a historical mission to accomplish. She repeats her warning: **"It is up to you, the workers who are in fact the victims of de-facto inequality, and injustice, it is up to you to reestablish on earth the rein of justice and absolute equality between men and women".**

According to Yolanda Marco: "We can define Flora as a thinker who, based on idealist assumptions framed within utopian socialism, upon analyzing reality does so in such an objective manner so as to empirically place herself within a materialist context. The conclusions that she arrives at therefore are much closer to scientific socialism than to utopianism". Later, "within her work, we think that we should emphasize the elements that directly match Marx's ideas and continue to only see the traits in common with social utopianism, as has been done. We think that the only criticism is that Flora Tristan's ideas are not systematic as they lack a dialectical materialism methodology that would organize them. If so, it is no less certain that the conclusions she reaches are **counter to social utopianism and belong to the world of basic principles of Marxist socialism".**

For Flora, the worker only owns his strength to work. The bourgeoisie is the owner of the means of production, the owners of the factories, the property owners, and land owners. Women conform to a different social group within the same bourgeoisie and the working class. Flora considers women to be an oppressed "race", oppressed by the very working class itself.

From this came her interest in convincing women that they should join men in the fight for their rights and convince the proletariat that without women's liberation they would never achieve their own liberation.

Flora Tristan's ideas coincide in general terms with Marx and Engel's ideas and with a series of points that have made numerous authors think about the possibility that the book "Promenade dans London" was known to Engels. The "Worker's Union" itself might have been read by Marx as his friend Ruge, who knew and visited Flora, could have brought it to him. Both Marx and Engels make reference in the book "The Sacred Family" and in "The Misery of Philosophy". Loyal to her statements in favour of the disinherited, Flora revives the Saint Simon defense on **rehabilitation and the sacredness of manual labour**. Flora claims "that rehabilitation itself involves society's radical change".

"Manual labour has always been and is still looked down upon. The only opinion in this regard is to consider manual labour degrading, shameful, and almost dishonorable for the one engaged it in. This is so true that the worker hides his laboring situation as he can, because he himself is humiliated. He who works with his hands sees himself disdainfully cast aside everywhere; this prejudice has infiltrated the customs of all peoples and is even found in their languages. Well, it must be agreed that in face of such a state of things, Mr. Enfantin has shown great strength and superiority in teaching his disciples to honor manual labor. After establishing the law, he wanted to enforce it.

So with the superior authority vested in him by his title of religious leader, he required his disciples to work with their hands, to mix among the workers, and to join them in the roughest and most repulsive trades".

With political acuity, Flora defends the salary of the future worker's defense before Parliament, because as she states "Now are the time to redistribute services according to their usefulness". Flora alludes to the slander and critiques of the bourgeoisie against O'Connell, the Irish people's defense. Flora says: "It is understandable that O'Connell's political enemies should adopt the tactic of heaping reproaches, insults, and slander upon him over the wages he receives from Ireland. Motivated by partisan hatred, the British aristocracy would like to defame O'Connell in the minds of the Irish to rid Ireland of its defender. Yet O'Connell's behavior is nothing but very loyal, legal, and in complete conformity with the rules established by a healthy morality". "You workers who earn a living by the sweat of your brow, don't you understand that all work deserves pay? Why shouldn't O'Connell, who works to bring Ireland out of slavery, receive the salary earned by his work? And what hard labor it is when a man gives his whole life to the defense of the popular cause! No more repose for him, as he is constantly preoccupied with seeking means of defense; day and night, he is always at work. What about the two million he receives? Can the life of the heart, the soul, and the mind be paid in gold? It is about time to remunerate services according to their usefulness".

This same defense by Flora is showing that he who works has the absolute right to receive a salary, without reducing his dignity, because it is just and deserved, because in the best of cases, the defense or the worker has the same needs as others to maintain his subsistence, as long as it does not deal with a person who is economically comfortably off or a public service institution without state funding. Also it is political to keep in mind that the person in charge will perform his/ her duties better the more fairly he/she is compensated, since he/she is without economic pressures of any kind. That this be within the socialist principles: *all work should be paid.*

CHAPTER VI

WOMEN'S RIGHTS

Flora never shows to be non-religious. In many of her expressions and statements she identified herself as a catholic and even a believer which didn't stop her from making precise and true comments about religion and women. In Chapter III of the "Workers Union" entitled: "Why I Mention Women" and justifying her role in awaking interest of the workers in defense of women, she says:

"Workers, you my brothers, for whom I work with love, because you represent the most vital, numerous, and useful part of humanity, and because from that point of view I find my own satisfaction in serving your cause, I beg you earnestly to read this with the greatest attention. For, you must be persuaded, it concerns your material interests to understand why when I mention women I always designate them as *female workers* or *all the women*".

And she continues later at her central theme of her thesis:

"Up to now, woman has counted for nothing in human society. What has been the result of this? The priest, the lawmaker, and the philosopher have treated her as a true pariah. Woman—one half of humanity—has been cast out of the Church, out of the law, out of society. For her, there are no functions in the Church, no representation before the law, no functions in the State. [1] The priest told her, 'Woman, you are temptation, sin, and evil; you represent flesh that is, corruption and rottenness. Weep for your condition, throw ashes on your head, seek refuge in a cloister, and mortify your heart, which is made for love, and your female organs, which are made for motherhood.

And when thus you have mutilated your heart and body, offer them all bloody and dried up to your God for

---

[1] Notes by Flora in "The Workers Union". Aristotle, less sentimental than Plato posed this question without answering it: Do women have a soul?" La Falange, August 21, 1842. Therefore, with three votes less, women would belong to the animal kingdom of irrationals and as man would be their owners they would have been obliged to cohabitate with an irrational animal. The author of Ecclesiastes carried the pride of his gender to the point of declaring: "A man with vices is worth more than a virtuous woman". Most wise men, whether they are naturalists, doctors or philosophers, have more or less concluded implicitly that women are inferior" "Woman was made for man" (St. Paul).

remission from the original sin committed by your mother Eve.' Then the lawmaker tells her, 'Woman, by yourself you are nothing; you have no active role in human affairs; you cannot expect to find a seat at the social banquet. If you want to live, you must serve as an appendage to your lord and master, man. So, young girl, you will obey your father; when married you shall obey your husband; widowed and old, you will be left alone.' Then the learned philosopher tells her, 'Woman, it has been scientifically observed that, according to your constitution, you are inferior to man. Now, you have no intelligence, no comprehension for lofty questions, no logic in ideas, no ability for the so-called exact sciences, not aptitude for serious endeavors. Finally, you are a feeble-minded and weak bodied being, cowardly, superstitious; in a word, you are nothing but a capricious child, spontaneous, frivolous, for ten or fifteen years of your life you are a nice little doll, but full of faults and vices. That is why, woman, man must be your master and have complete authority over you.'

Flora says: "So that is how for the six thousand years the world has existed, the wisest among the wise have judged the *female* race".

"Such a terrible condemnation, repeated for six thousand years, is likely to impress the masses, for the sanction of time has great authority over them. However, what must make us hope that this sentence can be repealed is that the wisest of the wise have also for six thousand years pronounced a no less horrible verdict upon another race of humanity: the proletariat. Before 1789, what was the proletarian in French society? a serf, a peasant, who was made into a taxable, drudging beast of burden. Then came the Revolution of 1789, and all of a sudden the wisest of the wise proclaimed that the lower orders are to be called the *people,* that the serfs and peasants are to be called *citizens*. Finally, they proclaimed the *rights of man* in full national assembly. The proletarian, considered until then a brute, was quite surprised to learn that it had been **the neglect and scorn for his rights that had caused all the world's misfortunes."** [2]

With a bit of irony, Flora reviews the period of the French Revolution, that in its Declarations of "The Rights of Man's and the Citizen" in 1793, doesn't leave the eyelet of hope with regards to women's participation in these declared Rights as outlined exclusively for men. Women continue to be in legal limbo, undoubtedly ignored or silenced by the same bourgeois society governed by men, who have no interest in women's liberation.

[2]   "Workers Union"

Bourgeois moral are hidden under avarice and hypocrisy. Women certainty lack the balance needed to open the doors of freedom and justice.

Flora researches the social ladder and only finds sincerity and purity in the most ignorant class, within its humble status, incapable of judging human behaviour. Because the famous human rights that are in place in the citizen life, is not an absolute given for the working class that in 1843 when Flora wrote this book, she still suffered the discrimination and exploitation of the capitalists. With political changes, women have been denied the right to divorce, a law that was current and for which re-establishment Flora forcefully petitioned Parliament.

As interpreted by Flora, the Revolution of 1789 was a bourgeois revolution, of which served the bourgeois deceiving the people and confusing them. Such as the independence of the Spanish domain to the countries of America, served for them to become established in their position of domination; the upper social class' progenies of the Colony, did not emancipate either the native, nor the black from their slavery.

Flora reflects: "The wealthy accuse the workers of being lazy, debauched, and drunk; and to substantiate their accusations, they exclaim, 'If the workers are miserable, it is their own fault. Go to the bars and taverns and you will find them filled with workers drinking and wasting their time' in the current state of affairs, the tavern is the worker's TEMPLE; it is the only place he can go. He does not believe in the Church; he does not understand anything about the theatre. That is why the taverns are always full. In Paris, three-quarters of the workers do not even have a home: they sleep in furnished barracks".

She continues: ". . . you do not want to teach the people, you forbid them to meet, in the fear that they will teach themselves or will talk of politics or social doctrines. You do not want them to read, write, or fill their minds with thoughts, for fear that they will revolt! So what do you expect them to do? If you prohibit everything that is mental, it is clear that, as a last resort, there remains only the tavern. Poor workers sometimes go crazy overwhelmed with misery and sorrows of all kinds at home or with their bosses, or finally because the repugnant and forced work to which they are condemned irritated the nervous system so much. In this state, their only refuge is the tavern, in order to escape from their suffering. So they go to drink blue wine, an execrable medicine whose virtue is the power of intoxication".

"Before such facts, there are people in the world called *virtuous* and *religious* who, comfortably settled in their homes, drink lots of good Bordeaux wine, vintage Chablis, and excellent champagne, at every meal, and those people make a beautiful moral fuss over drunkenness, debauchery, and intemperance in the working class! . . .

"In the course of studying the workers (I have been doing this for ten years), never have I encountered a drunkard or real debauched among happily married workers enjoying a certain ease. Whereas among those who are unhappily married, and deeply impoverished; I have found some incorrigible drunkards.

"The tavern, therefore, is not the cause of evil, but simply the effect. The cause of evil lies solely in ignorance, misery, and the brutalization of the working class. Instruct the people, and in twenty years the retailers of blue wine will close shop for lack of customers.

"Generally women of the masses are brutal, mean, and sometimes hard. This being true, where does this situation come from, so different from the sweet, good, sensitive, and generous nature of woman?

Poor working women! "They have so many reasons to be irritated! First, their husbands (It must be agreed that there are few working-class couples who are happily married) having received more instruction, being the head by law and also by the money he brings home, the husband thinks he is (and he is, in fact) very superior to his wife, who only brings home her small daily wage and is merely a very humble servant in her home".

"Consequently, the husband treats his wife with nothing less than great disdain. Humiliated by his every word or glance, the poor woman either openly or silently revolts, depending upon her personality. This creates violent, painful scenes that end up producing an atmosphere of constant irritation between the master and the (one can indeed say slave, because the woman is, so to speak, her husband's property). This state becomes so painful that, instead of staying home to talk with his wife, the husband hurries out; and as if he had no other place to go, he goes to the tavern to drink blue wine in the hope of getting drunk, with the others husbands who are just as unhappy as he. This type of distraction makes things worse. The wife, waiting for payday (Sunday) to buy weekly provisions for the family, is in despair seeing her husband spend most of the money at the tavern. Then she reaches a peak of irritation, and her brutality and wickedness redouble. You have to have personally seen these working-class households (especially the bad ones) to have an idea of the husband's misfortune and the wife's suffering. It passes from reproaches and insults to blows, then tears; from discouragement to despair".

"And following the acute chagrins cause by the husband come the pregnancies, illnesses, unemployment, and poverty, planted by the door like Medusa's head. Add to all that the endless tension provoked by four or five loud, turbulent, and bothersome children clamoring about their mother, in a small worker's room too small to turn around in. My! One would have to be an angel from heaven not to be irritated, not to become brutal and mean in such a situation. However, in this domestic setting, what becomes of the children? They see their father only in the evening or on Sunday. Always either upset or drunk, their father speaks to them only angrily and gives them only insults and blows. Hearing their mother continuously complain, they begin to feel hatred and scorn for her. They fear and obey her, but they do not love her, for a person is made that way—he cannot love someone who mistreats him. And isn't it a great misfortune for a child not to be able to love his mother! If he is unhappy, to whose breast will he go to cry? If he thoughtlessly makes a bad mistake or is led astray, in whom can he confide? Having no desire to stay close to his mother, the child will seek any pretext to leave the parental home. Bad associations are ease to make, for girls as for boys. Strolling becomes vagrancy, often becomes thievery.

"Among the poor girls in houses of prostitution and the poor men moaning in jails, how many can say, 'If *we had had a mother able to raise us, then we would not be here'*.

"I repeat, woman is everything in the life of a worker. As mother, she can influence him during his childhood. She and only she is the one from whom he gets his first notions of that science which is so important to acquire the science of life, which teaches us how to live well for ourselves and for others, according to the milieu in which fate has placed us"

There is no question that Flora's descriptions of working class life, which she was very familiar with, are completely factual and true, and not capricious inventions. One cannot try to convince the children of the masses with false or invented arguments for exactly what inspires Flora are their examples, painful, tragic, and even brutal. The sufferings that she was able to witness, in the people of the lower class of whose intimacy she had participated in for 10 years to penetrate their misery, their pain and their way of life. Also many of these experiences that she suffered herself when she was a vulnerable child and surely she knew hunger and shame, that led her to feel humble, abused and even worthless. When she had to face misery and chose to become a servant, a nanny, a traveling companion, or just a simple shop employee. These are her own experiences that inspire her and help her to convince the working class.

"In support of what I am maintaining here touching on women's brutality and the excellence of their nature, I shall cite an incident which occurred in Bordeaux in 1827 during my stay there:

"Among the vegetable vendors holding shop in the open market, there was one woman feared by all the good ones, for she was so insolent, mean, and brutal. Her husband was a garbage collector (which meant that he was a street cleaner and sewage gatherer). One evening he came home and supper was not ready. An argument ensued between the husband and wife. The husband wanted to get to the point with insults, and he struck his wife. At that moment she was cutting up morsels for the soup with a big kitchen knife, and she turned on her husband, piercing his heart. He collapsed, dead. She was taken to prison.

"Seeing her husband dead, this very brutal and wicked woman was gripped by such grief and remorse that, despite her crime, she inspired not only compassion but respect in everyone. It was simple to establish that her husband had provoked her, that the murder had been committed in a moment of anger, and not by premeditation. Her grief was such that one feared for her life; and since she was breast—feeding an infant of four months, the judge told her, in order to calm her, that she need not worry, she would be acquitted. But how surprised everyone was when, upon hearing those words, the woman exclaimed, 'Me acquitted! Ah! Your honor, what do you dare to say? If an awful woman like me were acquitted, there would be no justice on earth.'

"One tried everything to reason with her to make her understand that she was not a criminal, since she had not the thought of committing the murder. "Well! What does the thought matter?" she repeated, "if there is a brainless in me who can make me cripple one of my children or kill my husband? Am I not a dangerous person, incapable of living in society?" Finally, when she was quite convinced that she would be acquitted, this uneducated woman made a resolution worthy of the strongest men in the Roman Republic. She declared that she would take justice into her own hands and let herself starve to death. And with what strength and dignity she executed that terrible death sentence she imposed upon herself! Her mother, her family, and her seven children came and tearfully begged her to agree to live for them. She gave her small infant to her mother and said, "Teach my children to be glad to lose such a mother, for, in a moment of brutality, I could kill them as I killed their father." The judges, the priests, the market women, and many other from the town went to her and tried to solicit in her favor. She could not be moved. Then, another means was tried: cakes, fruit, dairy products, wine, and meats were brought to her room. Even some chicken was roasted and brought piping hot so the aroma would entice her to eat. "Everything you're doing is useless", she repeated with great coolness and dignity. "A woman who is brutal enough to kill the father of her seven children must die, and I will die". She suffered awful torment without complaining, and on the seventh day, she expired."

Flora considers it carefully: "In England where the working class is much more ignorant and miserable than in France, the working men and women carry the vice of drink as far as dementia."

"In the life of the workers, woman is everything. She is their sole providence. If she is gone, they lack everything. So they say, "it is woman who makes or unmakes the home," and this is the clear truth: that is why it has become a proverb. However, what education, instruction, and direction, moral or physical development do the working-class women receive? None.

"Nothing embitters the character, hardens the heart, or makes the spirit as mean as the continuous suffering a child endures from unfair and brutal treatment. First, the injustice hurts, afflicts, and causes despair; then when it persists, it irritates and exasperates us and finally, dreaming only of revenge, we end up by becoming hardened, unjust, and wicked."

In her invocation to men about the need to include woman in enjoying all rights, Flora affirms that the only way of to liberate *them from exploitation and misery* is having in mind that woman who is educated and conscious of her rights will be a better support in the workers action fighting for the working class. [1]

"Are you beginning to understand, you men, who cry scandal before being willing to examine the issue, why I demand **rights for women**? Why I would like women placed in society on a footing of **absolute equality** with men to enjoy the legal birthright all beings have?

"I call for woman's rights because I am convinced that all the misfortunes in the world come from this neglect and scorn shown until now for the natural and inalienable rights of woman. I call for woman's rights because it is the only

---

[1] "The Workers Union" Chapter 3 Flora Tristan. Editorial Fontamara, Barcelona. 1977

way to have her educated, and woman's education depends upon men in general, and particularly the working-class man's. l call for woman's rights because it is the only way to obtain her rehabilitation before the church, the law, and society, and this rehabilitation is necessary before working men themselves can be rehabilitated. All working—class ills can be summed up in two words: poverty and ignorance. Now in order to get out of this maze, I see only one way: begin by educating women, because the women are in charge of instructing boys and girls.

"Men always complain about the bad moods and the devious and silently wicked characters women show in all their relationships. Oh, would I have a very bad opinion of women, if in the state of abjection where the law and customs place them; they were to submit without a murmur to the yoke weighing on them! Thanks be to God, that it is not so! Their protest, since the beginning of time, has always been relentless. But since the declaration of the rights of man, a solemn act proclaiming the neglect and scorn the new men gave to women, their protest has taken on new energy and violence which proves that the slave's exasperation has peaked".

Around this theme so dear to Flora, she gives all kinds of examples about on workers so that they can understand without prejudice, the rights of women and her equality with men not to feel superior to them but to live in peace without suspicious or fears, to be equals, not servants or slaves nor to deserve man's contempt nor his authority and power. In order to sit an example for children, of understanding and tolerance that influence their will being and their future.

"In calling for justice, prove that you are just and equitable. You, the strong men, the men with *naked arms*, proclaim your recognition that woman is your equal, and as such, you recognize her equal right to the benefits of the *universal union of working men and women.*"

Flora dictates her statements to the workers that have to propose in order to achieve the laws that need to be written, demanding Women's Rights exactly as proclaimed in the Rights of Man and the Citizen in the Revolution.

Her feminism is so absolute that she does not to even call it that, not the reiteration of including women's rights in all of the chapters of her book "Workers Union", "because not doing it would assume a lack of care or forgotten".

It is as if she forgets herself or was conspiring against her own cause. Her experience is her incentive most powerful to insist until exhaustion that Women's Rights be maintained as a flag of redemption. *Absolute equity* men and women is the basic thesis of the UNIVERSAL UNION OF MEN AND WOMEN WORKERS.

That is how the First International of the working class without differences between sex, religion or nationality was generated.

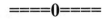

CHAPTER VII

FLORA TRISTAN'S PRIVATE LIFE

I have preferred to name this chapter this way, instead of adjectively label her love or sexual life that could very well correspond to her. We have to place our heroine in the ambience or ambient and the epoch of the times which she moved in during her short life as a social entity, and subsequently as a fighter and precursor of ideas and socio economic doctrines which were hardly outlined by the utopians and other thoughtful theorist's people of her time.

Flora the girl is a creature made haughty by her parents that enjoy comfort and affluence. As an orphan she is an abandoned creature in the midst of a hostile world, with a mother and a younger brother on whom the full weight of their misery lies, when the father passes away. All these can be blamed on the indifference of an uncaring father and the selfishness of her Peruvian relatives, who abandoned the bereaved family, and cast them against the most wretched conditions. They never pay any heed to the mother's letters to Uncle Pio, during the first years of her widowhood.

Society itself, the governing power of the 1808 epoch—the consulate-disregarding the despair that the family had been reduced to, instead of trying to assist them so they would not fall in the most dire poverty they strip the family of all their belongings and force them to run away aimlessly. First they roamed the fields; later they ended up in the Paris periphery where all the scum of society reside. All of these happened under the pretext that Mariano Tristan y Moscoso was still a subject of the Spanish King, and that France was at war with that country. The fact that the mother, Anne—Pierre Laisnay, was a French national was not taking into account, and the fact that the two children were born (out) or into of their marriage in France was not considered either, only the mentioned subterfuge mattered in the cruel dispossession.

To make matters worse, no doubt by instructions from Peru, the Peruvian Consulate in an inconceivable act, proceed to compile the files and information on Mr. Tristan, as non-embargo able items by the French Government, but never examined the documents to find any document as proof to the rights of the wife and two children. To the French eviction, the Spanish one was added without reflecting on the situation of the family of a single mother and two children. That is the way the laws of the land went in those days.

Very little is known about the family for the next fifteen years, when the young brother has already died, and Flora has lived through the nuisance of instability, poverty and the awareness of her doubtful legitimacy [1] of her Peruvian paternity. We have to think of an adolescence void of respects, drifting around the slums, struggling, her and her mother, for the bare necessities of life. Home business? domestic services? It is at this point that she gets the first notions of elemental culture. Her mother was a petit bourgeoisie, intelligent, of liberal ideas, that made her migrate to Spain, where she was received in the heart of society, where she met her future husband and many members of the Latin-American society, among them the America Liberator to be Simon Bolivar. [2] She also acquired knowledge of painting.

---

[1] According to the chronology of "La Union Obrera" published by Editorial Fontamara in 1977, Flora discovered in 1818 that her parent's marriage had not been legitimate.

[2] Most of Flora's biographies give little importance to the character of her mother, Ann-Pierre Laysnay. Nevertheless, she was a cultured woman who maintained a long correspondence with Simon Bolivar. Those letters are in the Pariah's bibliography as "Bolivar's Letters".

When she became homeless and had to seek refuge in the provincial fields, she opted to run to Paris. The joyful Paris that enjoys certain stability after the political activities, but a Paris that cannot give the roaming family other than what is proverbial to the impoverished women, in other words "the oldest feminine profession in the world" prostitution to survive. None of the biographers point to either the mother or the daughter as having resorted to such a process.

Flora is a beautiful girl and no doubt desired by the men that met her in those times. It is possible that she did lack sexual desire, because it is not in her adventures to go in the wrong direction even in defense of her own life which is border lining to the saddest poverty. In this way, it is noted her scarce love activity, perhaps as a measured condition to maintain a respectful image for social convenience sake.

Flora's sexual life starts, no doubt, when she weds Andre Chazal, when she is merely seventeen years old, perhaps not in love but pressured by the urgent needs and the mother's advice, to liberate herself of the extreme misery. It is possible that she received love happiness from this man in love with her, in the first years of marriage. L.A. Sanchez comes to this conclusion in his book "A

Lone Woman against the World" [1] with luxury of details, perhaps of his own invention. Sexual knowledge must have been an experience that fulfilled her desires as a woman.

The matrimonial separation must have happened very early. Since Flora does not receive her first two sons with the habitual motherly enthusiasm and as she is pregnant with her third child, she distances the husband, giving start to the persecution that shadows a great part of her youth. In these circumstances, and her perilous emotional stability, it is difficult to conceive a romance in her life, at least the biographers do not consign it as real, not leaving room for innuendo.

In her constant trips to London, as a nanny or tutor, there are no signs that Flora had any hidden romance. It does neither show, nor she makes mention of it, unless she wrote it mimetically in her novels or later writings.

The time she lived in Peru, approximately one year, she had friendly relationships with many men. Some of them besought a love relationship, among them the sailor Zacarías Chabrié, who proposed matrimony to her and promised to take her away from her suffering in Paris to a love nest in California. Although he was one of the few,

---

[1] L.A. Sánchez. "Una Mujer Sola Contra el Mundo". Córdoba, Argentina. 1942

that she demonstrated gratitude and affection to, rebuffed his proposals. She knew them impossible to happen, since she was a married woman.

Among her Peruvian admirers, a Peruvian consulate bureaucrat, Felipe Bertera, and Colonel Bernardo Escudero,—he was already in Peru—, and some others that put a little of warmth and affection in her life. However, they did not reach a more intimate relationship, no doubt, in order to maintain a respectable image before the Peruvian society and her own family, who would have judge her severely.

Physical love was very far from Flora's life, and there are examples that in this context place her as a sexually repressed woman-her marriage experience—or perhaps sexually frustrated, forced by a turbulent life. This theories explain her mood changes, isolation or reclusion that could be very well due to lack of sexual activity, so necessary for her own physical and emotional balance.

Nonetheless every assumption, there are true indications that Flora must have caused volcanic reactions in men at her return from Peru, particularly abate Alphonse Louis Constant—or Eliphas Leví as was known in circles of occultism-who was faithful even beyond her death. He developed such passion for the Pariah, that he wrote a book—while Flora was still alive—called "L'Assumption de la Femme, ou Le Livre de L'Amour". It was a collection of some semi-pagan psalms that praised her and insult at the same time, given the woman's impassivity: "Flora is the arrogant personification of the most wholesome and implacable pride. Milton's Satan must have died of despair since she came to the world, you have to know this woman to admire her and shudder."

Flora lived among men more than in the closeness of women, except in her stage of Messiah Woman. Men admired her and loved her, without getting involved romantically as lovers.

As Ventura García Calderón quotes, "there was not a woman from her time period who was more loved and admired in Paris". [1] Nonetheless, she merely knew what plentiful love was and how to enjoy it fully as a woman.

Flora was a spiritually solitary being, without deep affective roots, without the human presence of a shared love, without remission. Her two best admirers were: Paulina Roland, her follower in her pilgrimage and ideas, and Eleonora Blanc the humble woman who accompanied her until death. Artists, writers, poets, politicians, workers, made the frame of her best friends. Beautiful, intelligent,

---

[1] Ventura Garcia Calderon. "Nuestra Santa Aventurera"—Our Holy Adventure"—in Vale un Peru—Its Worth Peru—Paris. 1939.

passionate, Flora modeled for famous painters that were attracted to her beauty and her large sad eyes, captured in many portraits for posterity, which have been exhibited publicly among the world's most beautiful women.

Flora always regretted not having been a better mother to her children, which is only an excess of shame. She suffered like none other, protecting her children from their stalking father, who converted them in the object of his vengeance, and retaliatory hate for his wife. She fought and tried to hide them from their persecutor, pushing it to the public scandal many times she snatched them from the fathers hands and resorting to the law to force him to give them back. The time she resided in Peru was tormenting to her, since she could not receive any news from her children, in order to be able to conceal the fact that she was a married woman. Lastly, she was the victim of Chazal's fury when he shot her on the street leaving her for dead; defending her children.

At times when she was sick and bent down with so many misfortunes, her beloved Marie Aline, and her mere presence alleviated her sorrows, and returned the smile to her lips.

CHAPTER VIII

FLORA'S SOCIAL EXPERIENCE

It is unquestionable that the visits Flora made to London impressed to such extent, that one can affirm that was this city, in full industrial-capitalist advance, that became the school to her social experiences.

The first visits to this city left a great curiosity to go deeper into the workers lives, and get closer to the societists, the cartists or the Owenists. This was not an easy task, since she was the nanny to a British family that made her travel around several European countries without much freedom to herself.

On her way back from Peru, where she witnessed the slavery system still active, she renewed her visits to London. Flora made it a task to learn the closest possible the life and sorrows of the British working class, which according to her version the proletariat was exploited even harder than the French. She knows that the French workers have more free time to sing, socialize, and laugh. She could not see this in the British workers, who were subjected to permanent vigilance, without breaks and with tasks harder than what their physical capacity allowed them to do. This system led them to quickly fall ill and die at a tender age of about 30.

In her book "Promenade dans London", and later in the segment that she publishes under the title "The Monster City" she describes the horrors lived by the workers from the textile industry. She describes as well the foundry and the railroad workers, where the work load exceeds the human capacity.

Flora knows the slums where the workers live stacked up with their families, children and elders, where the continuous rainfalls through the leaky roofs to their beddings and belongings, filling the air with a tepid un—breathable atmosphere.

In her book "The Monster City", she says "It is necessary to have visited the manufacturing cities, see the worker from Birmingham, Manchester, Glasgow, Sheffield, and Staffordshire, etc. to have a just idea of their physical suffering and the lax moral conditions of this part of the population. It is impossible to judge the British worker condition comparing it to the French . . . Great part of them lack clothing, bedding, furniture, cooking elements, wholesome foods, sometimes the most basic potato. They are confined for 12 or 14 hours a day on low quarters where the air is tarnished by the residue from the cotton, wool, line, cooper, iron lead particles. From these oppressive conditions, and a bad nutrition they go straight to alcohol excesses. Most of them are emaciated, weak, rachitic, and with open wounds; many suffer from lung diseases and they all walk with their heads and eyes low, look feignedly askance.

Farther ahead in the showcase of injustice that is her book "Monster City"; she says 'Slavery is not the worst humane misfortune since I came to know the British proletariat".

PUBLIC WOMEN

Flora has penetrated the British powerful industry that in turn squeezes the life out of the workers, their families and their children. However, she has as well made incursions into the terrible world of the "Public Women", not precisely the ones from the lowest of society, but the ones that abound by the industrial-capitalist aristocratic zones, which are rich and lavish. She manifests that "I have never seen a public woman without quivering, moved by a sentiment of compassion for our society, without feeling loathing for their organizations and hate for the dominators that indifferent to all same and respect for humanity, to all love for their fellow man, reduce God's creation to such a degree off abjection. They degrade the woman beyond brutality!

"I understand the highwayman that rob the travelers and expose to go to the guillotine. I understand the soldier that constantly put his life at play and do not receive anything in return, but a few cents a day. I understand the sailors that expose their life against the seas fury. I understand the ones that find within their occupations a certain terrible dark poetry. However, I would not be able to understand the public women abandoning her, annihilating her will, her own feelings, offering her body to brutality and suffering, and her soul to contempt. I see in prostitution a horrible senselessness. To face death is futile, but what a terrible death the public women face! **Prostitution is the most horrific of the plagues that inequality on the world's resources distribution yields.** (We suggested the highlighting). This infamy withers the human species and attempts against the social organization even more than crime. If chastity had not imposed as a virtue to women, without compelling men, she would not be rejected by the society for consenting to the feelings of her own heart, and the seduced women would not be forced to go into prostitution.

"Virtue or vice is supposed to be the freedom to do good or bad, but what could be the moral standard for a woman that do not belong to herself, that do not have anything to herself, and that her whole life has been conditioned to be ready to fall into arbitrariness by shrewdness, and into duress by seduction. When women are tortured by misery, and when they see the enjoyment of wealth around men, when they sense the art of seduction in which they have been educated; are they not inevitably driven into prostitution?

Flora describes the neighbourhoods where the women of bad habits go in search of clients. It is very easy to tell them apart because there are so many and they are so foolish.

She went as an observer, accompanied by two friends armed with sticks and canes, to visit the area where they hang out. It was almost all covered by this type of women and their agents of prostitution. You go to this zone at night at the risk of your own life abuses from other thugs. The girls would pick out the windows, played around and exhibit themselves-nearly naked, or naked.

The spectacles that she was able to observe in the large "private rooms" of the high class filled her with horror and shame. She had the courage to witness men and women's physical and moral degradation in their lowest forms. It was her experience to confront the conscience of the inapprehensive British citizens, and that is the reason she wrote her "Promenades dans Londres" which was a sensation, followed by its excerpts, which she titled "Monster City." Only the ones that have read these books can compare the degree of degradation that the British Society of the industrial revolution, when great fortunes were invested in depravation and evil, and destroyed the impoverished women's dignity and lives. It was the poor ones that practiced that profession.

Flora describes the infamous white slaves trade. The way in which they are enrolled in the mafia, through work contracts, and once they were seduced, they were thrown into prostitution, and an assured death in a short time.

But the most painful aspect of prostitution, to Flora, was the fact that it was practiced with the youth, women as well as men. Girls were kidnapped as young as ten to fifteen, and the young boys were picked out in their adolescence, inducing them into sordid conducts and paying them at that early age, with total impunity for the culprits, even though their actions were penalized as crimes. All of these happened in spite of the existence of institutions that prevented and defended virtuosity and denounced vices. The sanctions were negligible compared to the vices.

Flora says: "depravation is extended to such heights and the prices they get for the deceived young girls are so high that there is hoax that they do not go to, to procure them".

This is, most likely the most painful experience in her trips to London, where she learnt how far the social injustice will go, and the exploitation of women, in this aspect of corruption and vice.

She met with "the 20 million of British proletariats", whose social inequity was far worse than the French ones, with salaries much lower, and subjected to a true slavery by the owners of the giant industrial-capitalist factories that made up the bourgeoisie of the times. It is very interesting the anecdote that she relates when she disguised herself as a Middle easterner, she walked into the British parliament session hall and proved to what point the public representatives had no idea about the miserable conditions in which the workers lived, because of the human exploitation by the privileged class. By then, women were not allowed inside the parliament to listen to the representative's discourses. Flora, at a particular time, stood up and started scolding the parliamentarians for the inhumane situation in which the working class was kept, men as well as women. The parliamentarians could not impede her intervention until she was taken out from the hall. Flora also had the opportunity to connect with the utopians, the Chartesians and the ones that pretended to alleviate the people's suffering, through social or institutional reforms of social welfare. She meets O'Connell in parliament and O'Connor. O'Connell is the Irish people's defender before the British public power. She is impressed by the Fuerists movement and their projected "Workers Palaces", over which scaffolding she will build later her social doctrine: THE WORKERS UNION.

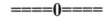

CHAPTER IX

SOME OPINIONS FOR AND
AGAINST FLORA

Despite the silence surrounding Flora Tristan for the last 100 years, many writers, sociologists, and researchers of social movements, name her in their works and even categorize her among the pioneers of socialist ideas who were threatened at the beginning of the last century. Some include her in the postulate of women's liberation.

We must note that the majority of the thinkers/ ideologists of her period either admired her or they refuted her. Many of them preferred to praise her beauty than her revolutionary vocation and ability. She created the first International organization of workers with her WORKERS UNION.

Among those who try to diminish the merits of the Woman Messiah is the English historian, G.D.H. Cole, the author of a work in seven volumes entitled "History of Socialist Thought" [1] in the first volume he cites Flora Tristan among the Utopists. This work, because of its breadth and content is compared to that of the historian Arnold Toynbee, since according to Gaston Garcia Cantu, its critic; it contains the full historic phenomenon: socialist thought. This is so, in effect, but with the exception that Cole, a man from the period 1889-1959, did not study the Precursor's personality more extensively as he did with the other famous persons from the period but bases his opinions on very dispersed documents of little truth, that existed a century after Flora Tristan disappeared.

There is no doubt that G.D.H. Cole barely read Flora's contemporaries and thought he places her between Luis Blanc and Lamennais in the section of the Pioneers from 1789-1850, he does not mention Flora's creation regarding the new concept of class that she catalogues the workers with, just like the bourgeoisie were called a class. Also, he appreciates a bit the announcement of Flora of creating a social conglomerate of political characteristics as was the Workers Union, with representation in parliament, in no way union or gremial. He also forgets to mention the great content of service and welfare that the so-called Workers

---

[1]   G.D.H. Cole. "Historia del Pensamiento Socialista"—History of Socialist Thought—. Fondo de Cultura Económica. 1962

Palaces embrace to alleviate the horrible abandonment of the sick, wounded, the elderly, or the men and women of the working class.

In Chapter XVII that he dedicates to her, he only makes one of the foundations of the "Workers Union" without analyzing the propositions that contain a social principle with solutions, maybe utopian for her time, but that were kept in mind by the socialists at little over 20 years. The Workers Union is a societal structure that states standards of action that are able to support the freedom of the working class from exploitation and misery that they are subject to.

G.D.H. Cole answers to equalizers thought, as he says he does not align himself with either the communists or the social-democrats but remains in the very centre of the proportions that he defines within the socialist concept.

With regards to women's liberation, the author states: "Until about the 19th century, no woman had an outstanding position in the development of socialist thought. The Saintsimonians never discovered women". Which is not exactly true since Saint-Simon was the follower of the doctrines of Fourier (1772-1837) who had said that "The level of women's liberation is the measure of that society's level of civilization".

Furthermore, feminist thought regarding women's liberation started many years before Cole's statement, when he says that there were not any thoughts of liberation in women, Mary Wollstonecraft the English feminist from the 18th century whose book "Vindication of the Rights of Women" Flora read in 1825 when she was recovering from the birth of her daughter Marie Aline, which awakened in her many ideas about the women's rights.

Certainly many other forgotten women, like Susan B. Anthony the North American born in 1820, and outstanding fighter for women's rights, were also inspired by Mary Wollstonecraft's book.

As well as those who, without calling themselves defender of women's rights, such as the famous Mexican poet Sor Juana Ines de la Cruz who was born in 1651, and who contempt men for accusing women of being morally light, since they are the ones who induce them. She calls them "foolish men."

In the two volumes work by Lewis L. Lorwin, entitled "History of the Workers Internationalism" [1] on page 28 of volume 1 there is a paragraph sub-titled:

---

[1] Lewis L. Lorwin. "Historia del Internacionalismo Obrero". Edicion Ercilla. Chile: 1934

"FROM FLORA TRISTAN TO KARL MARX"

That reads "Since 1843 onwards a persistent advance in the thoughts of 'intellectuals' and workers was produced also in their efforts to be able to establish a practical organization. In that year, in France there appeared a booklet called "The Workers Union" which expressed the first **complete plan for an international worker's organization.**

The author was Flora Tristan who had been strongly impressed by the Cartist movement in England and urged the workers in France to form themselves into a 'class' as the bourgeoisie had done in 1789 and 1830, so that they could join together without considerations of sex, political ideas, religion or country borders with the goal of being able to intervene in economic and political power."

Many years later the Marxist, Samuel Berstein, says of Flora "She is the first Utopian to show that the liberation of the working class can only be accomplished by themselves."

As Ventura Garcia Calderon says in his essay on Flora 'Our Saint Adventurer' [1] "Flora is the authentic founder

---

[1] Ventura Garcia Calderon. "Nuestra Santa Aventurera"—Our Saint Adventurer—in "Vale un Peru"—It's Worth Peru—Paris: 1939.

of the International, as her socialist comrade, Helen Brion, would realize".

Upon returning from Peru and having survived her family dramas, Flora enters the decisive phase of her life as a fighter for social justice. Unlike other utopists or utopian socialists, she looks deeper into the conditions of life for the working class both in London as Paris and in all of France Flora visits the most important intellectual and political people in her country as well as those she met in London during her many trips to that city. She had met Prosper Enfantin, a Saintsimoniano, and the societaria school that he professed, and with the first socialist trials of the Utopians. That was before her trip to Peru. After her return, she meets Fourier, Victor Considerant, the most renowned fourierista leader.

She makes friends with the famous poet Marceline Desbordes-Valmore, Robert Owen, the English cartist, the lawyer Duclos, Jules Laure who inspires her 'proletariat' in the book 'Mephis', later William Lowett, a Cartist and leader in those ideas, O'Connor and O'Connell, the defender of the Irish before the English parliament, Pauline Roland and Jeanne Deroin, founder of a feminist newspaper called "Women's Opinions". Among the famous intellectuals are Victor Hugo, Lamartine, Teofilo Gautier, Eugenio Sue,

Beranger, and the famous George Sand, whom she does not befriend because of their different characters yet, despite this, Sand is one of those who contributed to the first edition of her Workers Union. In her small hotel room in Paris, many famous people visit Flora who came to see her, attracted by her harangues and her suffering, those who would become her best sponsors in the idea of publishing her book. Up to three lists of subscribers exist for the three publications of Workers Union, the first with 4,000 copies and the last with 20,000. These lists have the names of the subscribers who include militaries, workers, teachers, housewives, domestic servants, deputies, a princess, artists, painters, musicians, priests, etc. etc.

Flora sent a copy of the first edition to the young and brilliant Karl Marx with his friend Ruge, Marx's collaborator.

Flora made additions to the second and third editions, reforming her arguments and adding her Marsellesas to the workers and the Workers Union. She was able to get Eugenio Sue to organize a contest to write the music for the worker's Marsellaise, which was won by the worker Thys.

Ahead of himself in March 1843, Victor Considerant publishes an extract from the "Workers Union" in his newspaper 'The Falange'.

FLORA TRISTAN'S EXTRAORDINARY INTUITION

Despite her personal experience, Flora never places women against men because she had already discovered and had declared that social inequality between men and women was the product of the operating system and that the same people who oppressed men, oppressed women. Nevertheless, she confirmed without a doubt by her own experience that in a class society, the workers men are the ones oppressing women. This discovery predates that of Marx and Lenin.

Likewise, Flora announced the brilliant phrase:

"The workers liberation will only be done by themselves".

These thoughts by Flora and her creation of the socio-political instrument, the First Workers International, the Workers Union reveal her quality of absolute novelty in a period when still the Historical Materialism did not appear, nor the Communist Manifesto that contains it, and which was published four years after the Precursor's death.

Her intuition is also extraordinary when she reclaim to the working class the full incorporation of women, who represent half of humanity, to the social struggle and as a form of secure the revolutionary action of the workers, men and women.

CHAPTER X

THE MESSIAH WOMAN

Having published the booklet 'Workers Union' [1] Flora decided that she should personally put it into all of the workers' hands across France. Thus was born in her head the idea of the "Tour de France", a tour through all of the industrial areas in the country to which she would take her oral and written message as she was sure of the great effect that direct action constitutes for exposing and explaining her propositions to the workers themselves, to whom the book is directed. The first edition of "Workers Union" had quickly run out in Paris itself and two further publications followed it, the last with 20,000 copies, to cover all of the area visited with more or less 25 million workers in all of the categories of work including the mines.

---

[1] The first edition of "L'Union Ouvriere"—The Workers Union—was published on June first, 1843.

The Pariah continues to churn in her mind the best way to impress the masses and achieve their understanding. Then she thinks of music. The hymns, popular songs exalting the valor of work and the desires for social improvement are a wonderful way to reach the understanding and the conscience of those at whom the Workers Union is directed. Flora visits the great writers of the period, Beranger and La Fontaine, Lamartine to ask them to compose the lyrics for 'The Workers Marsellaise' but it is to the workers themselves that she convinces that they should write it themselves, facing the difficulties that the named writers presented, they do not refuse. They felt inept to do it. So, anonymous workers compose the two songs that later would be incorporated into the successive editions of the Workers Union.

Meanwhile, Eugenio Sue, one of Flora's admirers organized a contest to compose the music for "the Workers Marsellaise" and the worker composer Thys won the accolade.

Flora plans her tour that she thought could begin in the month of December. She decides that she should be the one to teach the singing of the 'Workers Marsellaise' and the 'Hymn of the Workers Union' that were born almost simultaneously.

'TOUR DE FRANCE'

Her hoped-for tour did not begin until April 1844. The sale of her book was a success and in the following editions, the third and fourth, she included the letters from her friends congratulating her on her work as well as the lyrics for the two 'Marselleisas'. Each edition was augmented with new initiatives, statements, and stimulus on the advantages of the union for male and female workers. She insists on convincing them that only the union *of the most useful and exploited class* will save them from their misery [1].

In the cover of the third edition, Flora published:

UNION OUVRIERE
par
Mme. FLORA TRISTAN
TROISIEME EDITION
contenant
LA MARSEILLAISE DE L'ATELIER
mise en musique

---

[1] The first edition of "L'Union Ouvriere" had a run of 4,000 copies the second had 10,000 and the third 20,000. Flora received economic assistance from many friends and admirers. This information is from the French edition of "L'Union Ouvriere" that was published in Lyon on June 7, 1844

par A. THYS

Paris et Lyon

1844

Chez Tous les Libraires

In each edition, Flora publishes new collaborators with the amounts contributed by each.

Flora begins her tour with just the company of her fervor and her faith in the ideals in her book 'The Workers Union'. She wants to make it the best instrument for fighting in the hands of the working class. She travels with elemental clothing given her economic situation and her desire not to add to the cost of the trip anything that could affect the work to be performed. Her apparel was modest without paying attention to the weather, rain or sunshine. Her shoes were not adequate for the marches that she has to endure to get to the workers in their own places of work, factories shops, and construction sites. Flora falls ill several times. The pariah's health is truly precarious, tortured by the continuous suffering, struggles and persecutions. All that is strong in her is her will power, her fighting character, and her tenacious determination to root bases to a social organization that cover all workers in France and around the world; with its powerful drive the working class will not be exploited any more.

Her journeys consume her days and nights, and many are the obstacles on the way many caused by hindsight. The workers distrust her, sometimes because she is a young and beautiful woman, some other times because she is not backed up by a union or organization. All of these added to the fact that she talks a daring and liberal language, which is unusual for women of the epoch; she understands, but such is her vehemence that she reaches their attention. She is heard and treated with respect.

Flora promotes meetings at the hotel where she stays, she explains the contents of her brochure, lobbies financial cooperation from the workers in small yearly donations, but that added together will yield a fabulous amount that will be used to carry out the WORKERS UNION projects. She talks to women showing them the inequality in which they find themselves even within their own working class; she let them see that their work is worth less than men's, and not paid well; she let them see the sad condition that their children live in, going hungry, mistreated, dirty, because of their misery. After the meetings, she would teach herself them to sing the "Marsellaise of the Workers".

On one side of things, she cannot find adhesion to her ideas, the ones that she wants to save argue with her, make fun of her, or believe that she is an impostor. On the other side, they are moved by the Pariah's words, they promote salary grievances, give out protesting harangues, they organize strikes. All of these generate an open preoccupation in the social atmosphere of France amid the industrial-capitalist circles. The Police in alerted and Flora is watched along her tour. The Police goons raided her hotel room, but all they found is her books of "WORKERS UNION". She is labeled social agitator, feminist, and communist. She is called with all the qualified adjectives that the world's powerful class has come up with for the first insurgents of the socialist movement.

Flora has started her tour of Bourgogne, but her goal is to visit all the industrial zones of France. Her vehemence is more demanding, because she can feel the physical exhaustion closing in, time is short, and she must fulfill her proposed plans.

The nickname of Woman Messiah has replaced the Pariah, and this nickname is more appropriate since her solidarity mission has a social content. She preaches by example, since she considers herself a true worker. Her children are workers and nobody like herself has penetrated as profoundly as herself in the social layers of the workers world. She has shared with the British and French workers her table and their misery. She has even assimilated their popular jargon. She comprehends them and wants to be comprehended by them, but the great obstacle is the extreme ignorance, particularly among women, which makes them doubt and make them suspicious of her. Women workers feel odd with the Pariah's preaching, when she talks about getting closer to the workers organizations and their advantages, when she harangues that the women should take a more responsible role in those organizations. She continues pressing forward so not even a crack is left alone in her preaching of the **men and women workers union,** to strengthen the institution of the working class.

Flora lacks all kinds all comforts, she sleeps in cheap hotels, and money is scarce, even to cover the demands of the tasks to undertake. Her health diminishes; she has aged greatly. Perhaps in her sleepless nights she might be invaded by a tremendous feeling of frustration or failure because of the incomprehension from the workers. The very next day she would be back to her pledged lectures and nobody will impede her from risking her own health and life. She is full of faith and hope that she will finally be able to awaken the slumbering conscience of the French workers, and with that the rest of Europe.

Her enemies come together to attack her, many reproach her; they accuse her of lacking the capacity and authority to carry the task that she has undertaken. The majority consider her an utopian without any socialist content. But nobody adopts the ways she has walked to make contact with the working masses, in other words, with the root itself of proletariat, to learn their condition of inhuman exploitation by the bourgeoisie class. Male and female sufferers listen to her with more enthusiasm and interest, because she interprets their most inner suffering, their ancient miseries, their hunger, their fear. She speaks up for the ones that cannot. She is discovering, for them, a world that is possible to get to by way of joining forces.

Flora finds out that her project of **Workers Union** starts to be shared by many, except that they do not identify with the postulates because they share much of the utopians that base their aspirations on a happiness shared by all through cooperatives. The superstructure is missing, the doctrine no doubt. However, she has no interest on that. Her social conception is the **Workers Union** as a class in antagonism with the bourgeoisie class. The workers of any place are majority, they add to millions—20 millions in France, 25 millions in London—many more than the bourgeoisie class and the capitalists. The workers are therefore the true force without them nothing will develop, and nothing can be built up: the factories, the mines, the railroad, and the looms. Nevertheless while capitalists make enormous fortunes, the workers mere miserable salaries and live malnourished within the worst despair. Is it not the Union the gel that agglutinates those potential forces? She knows that she is right. Nevertheless the others know that as well that is not so simple to proclaim the union of all workers around the globe. There is still a long way to go. Flora thinks that all that is fine, however only theory. Action and thought must go together; the action must be tied to the word.

Union must be the first word, because union is power, and power is the goal.

Flora thinks that it is there where the triumph of the working class resides. She does not want to concede that there are other discrepant forces, the army. She knows them well enough, but they also belong to the exploited class. They are servers of the powerful enemy, and they become enemies, but they have to be convinced; make them understand. It has to be done. Nobody will convince her that the constant preaching, the true words will convert the enormous and disarmed army of the working class in an indestructible force able to conquer their own happiness.

The Woman Messiah is 41 years old. Time has run swiftly; her dreams neither are realized, but she takes a glimpse at smiles of understanding and affection among the men and women workers that she visits. As well the notoriety of her proselytism tour is well known throughout France. Lyon, Burdeoux Marseilles, Monptelier, Toulouse, Dijon, Chalon. She does not know how many places she has visited. In Marseilles she has entered the mining craters of

Roune, Saint Etienne. She has seen the way they work in darkness and submerged in water, hundreds of feet below the surface.

In Lyon, Flora meets the one that will be her spiritual daughter, who will accompany her to her grave, the faithful Eleonore Blanc. In Burdeoux has accomplished the installation of a Union committee. She goes back to some places, where she hints the possibility to secure a base for the **Workers Union**. Her books are either sold, or given to the workers after her teachings about their meaning. They all know her ideas, or start to know them and hum her songs. At some bypassing ports, strikes ignite, mutinies break out, and sabotages develop. The agitator is blamed for everything. The workers defend her; it is not her but the working conditions, the inhumane exploitation that they are subjected to, what causes the revolt.

In Paris the Bauer brothers, Hegelians, attack her. They point at her as dogmatic, the main women's defect, according to them. In Lyon as she is saying farewell to a crowd she heard with emotion the workers singing the Workers Marsellaise. How could she put in doubt the workers class awakening?

This and other manifestations of controlled adhesion and affection, balance, and encourage her to continue her march around France. Her tour is stretching into the eight months. Has happened so fast, just enough to reach, and iron the wrinkles from the brow of those less comprehensive, of the women, and at the same time increase the police's watchfulness.

Her health is seriously aggrieved. The frugality she has submitted herself to by the circumstances, the excessive work load, and her vehemence have eroded the woman's fragile energy.

Her biographers consigned that at that point she was declared a social danger by the Police, and is followed to every place that she goes to; thus, the fearful owners of hotels and pensions along the way refuse to give her shelter. In her last trip to Burdeoux, Flora falls gravely ill. She falls into either delirium or unconsciousness for several days. On the 14 of November 1844 her sickness becomes critical, and the Pariah, the Woman Messiah, the tireless fighter, the creator of Workers Union, dies without regaining consciousness. She has had a long agony. She was living at the time in the home of the Saint-Simonians, Elisa and Charles Lemonnier. She is surrounded by her faithful Eleonora Blanc and many workers men and women that had comprehended her message. Burdeoux was her last port of call. She will rest there definitively.

Was it mission accomplished for the Pariah, did she sow the ideas of unity and social solidarity? The workers themselves voice it by raising, by public suffrage, a plain tombstone in the Chartreux cemetery, which inscription says:

To the Memory
Of Madame Flora Tristan
Author of the Workers Union
The grateful workers
Liberty, Equality, Fraternity
Solidarity
Flora Tristan born in Paris
On the 7 day of April of 1803
Died in Burdeoux, the 14 day of
November of 1844
Solidarity

In 1848, four years after her death, Marx and Engels, published their "Communist Manifesto" in which the fundamental ideas of the Workers Union of Flora Tristan are contained. 'The Manifest' many times corrected, will end with the warning invocation of the "Workers Union": Proletarians from all over the world, Unite!

This is the poor's people catechism, and at the same time, it is a way to recognize that the great social fighter that lived in Flora did not chose the wrong path. She only set herself forward in time. It was not the time yet, but it was very close.

Flora never forgot that the fight for women's emancipation was part of the social struggle, since she was herself part of that exploited class. That is the reason why she insisted that women workers should be included in the WORKERS UNION as well as men. That is the reason she wrote "Women's Emancipation" or "The Pariah's Will"

She was self taught in the best sense of the word; she had a vast knowledge, and an immense humanistic culture, acquired in her contacts with the intellectuals of the time, from her trips around Europe, and her enormous desire to know. As a writer, she collaborated in different magazines as a means of communication, plus to help herself financially with her own and her children's needs. Her books and publications are written under a social context to serve the needy, they are not literary productions created by her inspiration or fantasy. Her book "Mephis" or "The Proletariat" was catalogued as biographical, because it echoes a lot of her suffering under the husband's tyranny. "Peregrinations of a Pariah" is a collection of her notes and experiences on her trip to Peru, since the moment she leaves France to stay in Arequipa and Lima, which was her father's land. This book does not seem to be written by a literary amateur, but by an experienced writer. Furthermore, Flora creates, perhaps without trying, the **biographical novel style**. [1] All that was written by the Pariah translates her social critical view, her psychological deepness, her great intuition, her great sensibility to capture the phenomena of her times, and the contradictions of the bourgeoisie which were announcement of class conflicts that Flora underlined.

Her path is not snobbish or exhibitionist. It is the desire to acquire the necessary knowledge and experience to route her action to the service of the men and women workers. Her work was not just theory. She was an activist, to use todays term, because she was part of the scenario formed by the ones she wanted to awake from their atrophy and ignorance. She talked their language, she identifies with them to get their trust, their adhesion.

The woman Messiah could be catalogued as Exceptional, because it is hard to find a paragon like her persona full of intelligence and courage, in spite of all her personal suffering borderline to violent, which could not stop her or diminish her; au contraire, it made her stronger renewing her strength to continue fighting. Her strength did not take as far as she wanted to go, which was to make her dream come true, and achieve the installation of the infrastructure

---

[1] Jorge Basadre. Ob. Cit.

to the MEN AND WOMEN WORKERS UNIVERSAL
UNION. The historian G.D.H. Cole says, "Flora's ideas
died with her", without perceiving that the "Communist
Manifesto" contains them in its fundamental tenets. By
the same token, the "WORKERS UNION" is based on the
universal merging of the working class.

More than one hundred sixty years after she passed
away—1844—, Flora Tristan has resurrected. Her ideas
and her books proliferate in French libraries, and her name
is symbol and guidance for the fighting women that have
picked up her message of women's emancipation.

The Precursor's thought is almost institutionalized;
it is known and admired in the majority of countries
around the world, industrialized as the ones in process of
development.

There are several projects to bring her life to the movies,
which would end with the silencing of her story, and the
proscription of her name. It would return her stature of
fighter, heroine, authentic defender of the rights of the
working class in general, and women in particular.

We owe, then to this illustrious compatriot the
recognizing of her merits and give her in Peru the place that
she deserves as a representative of the Peruvian women,
together with the women that have done so much good to

our genre and Peru, for their deeds and sacrifices, done without any demand, search for a stardom or fame.

Flora should be remembered in the day of her birth, as our flag bearer as are the New York's martyrs—1857—subsequent to Flora.

It would be the best way to break the silence that has weighed over her name, as possible retaliation from all of those that she might have pointed on their defects and injustices, the ones that constitute the antagonist class to the workers. It is possible that no other woman like the Pariah, with the fighting vocation that took her to her grave, ever existed.

Flora died in her right, and left us such an exemplary lesson like no other one, only comparable to the heroines that died en defense of the liberty of our peoples. Such Micaela Bastidas. [1]

---

[1]   Micaela Bastidas: Born in Abancay, Sur del Peru, 1744-1781. At 15 years old she married Cacique Jose Gabriel Condorcarqui-Tupac Amaru II—and had three sons: Hipolito, Mariano and Fernando. In 1780 she led, along with Tupac Amaru, the great anticolonial rebellion in an effort to topple the bad government, the unjust fiscal reforms and abuses against natives. The uprising failed, she was captured and taken to Cuzco, where she was sentenced to be strangled. Her executer cut her tongue and; pull her neck, and as she was dying she was kicked in the stomach and chest. The same day her sons and husband were cruelly executed.

WORKERS UNION

PART TWO

**TO THE MEN AND THE WOMEN
THAT EXPERIENCE
FAITH—LOVE—INTELIGENCE
POWER—ACTIVITY**

TO WORKING MEN AND WOMEN [1]

"Listen to me. For twenty-five years the most intelligent and devoted men have given their lives to defending your sacred cause. [2] In their writings, speeches, reports, memoirs, investigations, and statistics they have pointed out, observed and demonstrated to the government and the wealthy that the working-class, in the current state of affairs, is morally and materially placed in an intolerable situation of poverty and grief. They have shown that, in this state of abandonment and suffering, most of the workers,

---

[1] PH-D Beverly Livingston, translator of "The Workers Union" III edition. University of Illinois Press, Chicago. 1983

[2] Henri de Saint—Simon, Owen, Fourier, and their Schools. Alexandre Parent-Duchatelet, Eugene Buret, Louis-Renée Villermé, Pierre Leroux, Louis Blanc, Gustave de Beaumont, Pierre Joseph Proudhon, and Etienne Cabet. Among the workers were Adolph Boyer, Agricol Perdiguier, Pierre Moreau, etc.

We are glossing the text from the Spanish edition of "La Union Obrera"- The Workers Union"- Editorial Fontamara, Barcelona, 1977 and the French original published in Paris in 1842-1843.

inevitably embittered through misfortune and brutalized through ignorance, become dangerous to society. They have proven to the Government and the wealthy that not only justice and humanity call for the duty of aiding them through a law on labor organization, but that even the public interest and security imperiously demand such a measure. Well, for the last twenty-five years, so many eloquent voices have not been able to arouse the Government's concern regarding the risks to society with seven to eight million workers exasperated by suffering and despair, with many trapped between suicide and thievery!

"Workers, what can be said now in defense of your cause? In the last twenty-five years, hasn't everything been said and repeated in every form? There is nothing more to be said, nothing more to be written, for your wretched position is well known by all. Only one thing remains to be done: *to act by virtue of the rights inscribed in the Constitutional Charter.*

"Now the day has come when one must act, and it is up to you and only you to act in the interest of your own cause. At stake are your very lives . . . or death, that horrible, ever-menacing death: misery and starvation.

"Workers put an end to twenty-five years of waiting for someone to intervene on your behalf. Experience and facts inform you well enough that the Government cannot or will not be concerned with your lot when its improvement is at issue. It is up to you alone, if you truly want it, to leave this labyrinth of misery, suffering, and degradation in which you languish. Do you want to ensure good vocational education for your children and for yourselves, and certainty of rest in your old age? You can.

"Our action is not to be armed revolt, public riots, arson, or plundering. No, because, instead of curing your ills, destruction would only make them worse. The Lyons and Paris riots have attested to that. You have but one legal and legitimate recourse permissible before God and man: THE UNIVERSAL UNION OF WORKING MEN AND WOMEN.

"Workers, your condition in present society is miserable and painful: in good health, you do not have the right to work; sick, ailing injured, old, you do not even have the right to care; poor, lacking everything, you are not entitled to benefits, and beggary is forbidden by law. This precarious situation relegates you to a primitive state in which man, living in nature, must consider every morning how he will get food for the day. Such an existence is true torture. The fate of the animal ruminating in a stable is a thousand times better than yours. He, at least, is certain of eating the next day; his master keeps hay and straw for him in winter.

"Then why do you remain isolated from each other? Individually, you are weak and fall from the weight of all kinds of miseries. So, leave your isolation: unite! Unity gives strength. You have numbers going for you, and numbers are significant.

"I come to you to propose a general union among working men and women, regardless of trade, who reside in the same region, a union which would have as its goal the CONSOLIDATION OF THE WORKING CLASS and the construction of several establishments (Worker's Union palace), distributed evenly throughout France. Children of both sexes six to eighteen would be raised there; and sick or disabled workers as well as the elderly would be admitted.

"You are going to say to me, 'but how do we unite for this great project? Because of our job situations and rivalries, we are all dispersed and often are even enemies at war with each other. And two francs yearly is a lot for poor day workers!'

"I shall respond to these two objections: uniting for the accomplishment of a great project is not associating. Soldiers and sailors, who each contribute equally through withheld wages to a common fund to take care of 3,000 soldiers and sailors at the Hotel des Invalids, are not associates for that reason. They do not need to know one another, nor have similar opinions, tastes, or personalities. All they need to know is that from one end of France to the other all the military contribute the same amount, which assures the right of admission to the hospital for the wounded, sick, and aged.

"As for the amount, I ask, who among the workers, even the poorest, cannot manage to save two francs in the course of a year to assure a place for retirement in his old age?"

However, Flora knows the indolence which the working class lives in, that is why she utilizes all methods to convince them. She dramatizes, curses, vociferates about the state of ignorance and ineptness in which the people, men and women lies in? Their mental blindness their foolishness and deliberately she hurt the most profound feelings of any human being, to wrench a slight of dignity or shame. She wants to shake them with her vehemence; she knows they are defenseless, incapable, clumsy, cowards. Even though there have been so many manifestations of insurgency that produced so many transformations—1789, 1830, and 1833—The Human and Citizen Rights have been declared. Every citizen enjoys the same rights, as the bourgeoisie but, is this reality? Perhaps the worker, the women from the working class enjoy the benefits from their own work? No, the working class continues tied to the will of the factory owners, they continue working 12 hour shifts that oppress and consume their force, their pay do not change, and the struggle to obtain better salaries only drive to a strike engagement with consequences like 1833, and the sequel of violent repression, and greater reprisals from the exploiters. Are not the workers the perpetual pariah of the bourgeoisie society? The barriers are not broken, only the repression methods have changed. The rich continues been rich, and the poor continues submerged in the most abject poverty.

Flora knows it well, the working class, the most useful class in the society, will always be exploited, as long as they do not become a powerful union, and as long as they continue in the ignorance. The bourgeoisie class will continue exploiting them, unless the workers create their own defenses, unless they unite to impose their conditions.

She says: "Yes, champions of labor, it is up to you to be the first to raise your voices in honor of the only truly honorable thing—work. Producers, scorned by those who exploit you, it is up to you first to build a palace for your worker's retirement. You who are builders of palaces for king and the rich, of God's temples and asylums to shelter mankind, it is finally up to you to construct a haven where you can die in peace. Otherwise you have only the hospice, and then when there is room. So, to work, to work!

"Workers, think about the effort I have just made to enable you to leave behind your misery. If you do not answer this call for unity, if through selfishness or lack of caring you refuse to unite, what can be done to save you in the future?

"Brothers, striking the heart of all those who write for the people is the distressing thought that, as of a young age, the poor are so abandoned and so overworked that three-quarters of them do not know how to read and the other quarter does not have time to read. So, to write a book for the people is like throwing a drop of water into the sea. That is why I realized that limiting my plan for a **Universal Union** to paper, as magnificent as it is, would create a dead letter, as had happened to so many others plans previously proposed. I realized that, with my book published, I had another task to accomplish, *which is to go from town to town and from one end of France to the other with my union plan in hand to speak to those workers who do not know how to read or have no time to read. I told myself that the time had come to act.* And for the one who really loves the workers and wishes to devote body and soul to their cause, there is a beautiful mission to fulfill.

"The workers have often been spoken of in the legislature, from the Christian pulpit, in society gatherings, on the stage, and especially in the courts. But no one has yet tried to speak to them. This had to be attempted. The Lord tells me it will succeed. That is why I am so confidently embarking on a new path. Yes, I shall go and find them in their workshops, in their attics rooms, and even in their taverns, if necessary. And amidst their very misery, I shall convince them about their own fate and force them, in spite of themselves, to escape the terror of that degrading and fatal poverty".

In this way, the Woman Messiah fulfilled her apostolate with a new faith, **the Universal Union of the Men and Women Workers**; The pariah that had declared her doctrine on her return from Peru, after the disappointing experience in her father's nation :

"From this point forward, my homeland will be humanity".

FLORA ANALIZES
WELFARE SOCIETIES, GUILDS ASSOCIATIONS

"While reading the *Book on Compagnonnage* by Agricol Perdiguier (a cabinetmaker), a little pamphlet by Pierre Moreau (locksmith), and the "Plan to Regenerate the Guild System," by Monsieur Gosset, master blacksmith, I was struck and enlightened by this great idea of the *Universal Union of Men and Women Workers.*

"In this three rather remarkable but small works the question of workers is envisioned by workers, intelligent and conscientious men, who are thoroughly familiar with the subject. The three works are thought out and written in good faith; ardent and sincere love for humanity can be felt on every page, precious qualities not always encountered in the learned works written by our famous economists.

"After showing us the guild system as it is today, the three worker writers proposed significant reforms for the various guild groups (Moreau in particular), each according to his character and way of seeing things. These reforms could doubtless improve the worker's habits; but, I must say, what struck me was seeing that, among the improvements proposed by Perdiguier, Moreau, and the father of blacksmiths, none was of the caliber to bring about a veritable, positive amelioration in the physical and psychological condition of the working class. In fact, let us suppose that all these reforms might be realized. Let us suppose that, according to M. Perdiguier's **wish the guild members no longer fought among themselves;** that according to M. Moreau's design, discrimination among trades disappeared to form a General Union; and that according to the master blacksmith's desire guild members were no longer exploited by the mother's. [1] Indeed, these would be lovely results. But, I ask, how would these reforms change the precarious, miserable situation of the working class? In no way, or at least very little.

"I do not know how to explain why these three workers writers, who so brilliantly pointed out small, specific reforms, did not think to propose a plan for a *universal union* whose goal would be to put the working class in a social position to demand its right to work, its right to education, and its right to be represented before the country.

For it is very clear that that is where all the other improvements would naturally come from. This very important lacuna in these three writings made a deep impression upon me. That is when I was enlightened by the great and beautiful notion of **the universal union of working men and women.**

"In thinking about the causes of the abuses and ills of all sorts pointed out by the workers writers, I saw where the evil came from and instantly understood what remedy can be applied. *Isn't poverty the true cause, the only cause* of all the evils afflicting the working class?

---

[1] 'Mother' is a tavern owner who gave credit to the workers when they were waiting to be paid.

"Yes, it is poverty, and because of it, the working class is condemned forever to wallow in ignorance, degradation, and enslavement. So poverty must be fought; it is the most redoubtable enemy!

"In my opinion, anyone who sincerely wants the real and effective improvement of **the most *populous* and *useful* class** [1] can propose only an easily and simply implemented means to give the working class the opportunity of leaving its precarious state gradually and nonviolently. And I have just proposed this means which is easy to implement and promises to be effective.

HOW TO CONSOLIDATE THE WORKING CLASS

"It is very important for the workers to distinguish between the Worker's Union as I conceive of it and what exists today under the titles of guild associations, the Union, welfare societies, etc. The goal of all these various private groups is simply to give aid, mutually and individually, within each society. Thus they were set up to

---

[1] Flora is surprised that the Saint—Simonans refer to the working class as the "poor class". She calls them the "most useful class" because they cooperate without question in the service of society's classes.

provide in case of sickness, accidents, and long periods of unemployment.

"Given the working class's current state of isolation, desertion, and misery, these kinds of societies serve a purpose. For their aim is to give a bit of aid to the most needy, thereby mitigating some personal suffering, which often surpasses the strength and stamina of those afflicted. So I highly approve of these societies and encourage the workers to increase them and get rid of the abuses they may have. But alleviating misery does not mean destroy it; mitigating the evil is not the same as eradicating it. If one really wants to attack the root of evil, obviously one needs something other than private societies, since their only goal is to relieve individual suffering.

"Let us examine what happens in the private societies and see whether this mode of action can actually improve the lot of the working class. Each society uses its membership fees to give so much per diem (between 50 centimes and 2 francs) to the sick and in some cases to those who have been out of work for a certain length of time. If, by chance, something happens, such as a member's being sent to prison, aid is available up to the time of the verdict.

"To boost their morale, each member of the association makes it his duty to go and visit sick members in their homes or in the hospital, and prisoners, as well. I repeat, given the current state of affairs, these sorts of groups are at least very useful in showing great sympathy and in binding the workers, for they encourage good morals, civilize their customs, and alleviate their awful suffering. But is that sufficient? No! Indeed not, since in the final analysis these groups cannot (and do not claim to) change or improve in any way the material and moral condition of the working class.

"A father belonging to one of these associations suffers miserably, and finds no solace in believing that his sons will be any better off than he. And in their turn, his sons as members of the same association will live miserably like their fathers, with no hope for their children. Mind you, each society acting in the name of the individual and trying to provide temporary relief invariably offers the same thing. Despite all its efforts, it will be able to create nothing great, good, or capable of notable results. [1] Therefore, Workers, with your private societies as they have existed since the time of King Solomon, the physical and psychological condition of the working class will not have changed in fifty centuries: its fate will always be **poverty,**

---

[1] During Christianity, millions of charitable groups have existed to lighten the load of the poorest. Despite their good intentions, the poor class has continued to exist, and gets poorer over time.

ignorance, and slavery, the only change being the types and names of slaves.

"What is wrong? This kind of absurd, selfish, mean, bastard organization divides the working class into a multitude of small private groups, the way large empires, which we see today as so strong, rich, and powerful, were divided during the Middle Ages into small provinces, which in turn were further divided into small towns with their own rights and freedoms. Well, what rights! That is to say, the little towns and provinces, continually at war with each other (and today war is competition), were poor, weak, and had as their only right the ability to moan under the weight of their wretchedness, isolation, and the terrible calamities inevitably resulting from their divisive state.

"So I am not afraid to repeat that the fundamental vice which must be attacked from every point is the system of separation, which decimates the workers and can only foster abuse. I think this short analysis will suffice to enlighten the workers about the true cause of their ills-division.

"Workers, you must leave behind this division and isolation as quickly as possible and march courageously and fraternally down the only appropriate path—**unity**. My union plan rests upon a broad base, and its spirit is capable of fully satisfying the moral and material needs of a great people.

"What is the aim and what will result from **the universal union of working men and women**? Its goals are**:**

1. To establish the solid, indissoluble unity of the working class;
2. To provide the Worker's Union with great capital through the optional membership of every worker;
3. To acquire a real power backed by this capital;
4. By means of this power, to prevent poverty and eradicate abuse by given working-class children a solid, rational education which will make them educated, reasonable, intelligent, and able men and women in their work;
5. To remunerate labor as it ought to be, generously and fairly.

"This is too beautiful!" one will cry. "It is too beautiful; so it is impossible".

Readers, before surprising your feelings and imagination with the icy words, **'it is impossible'**, remember that France has between 7 and 8 million workers, and with a membership of two francs each, that makes 14 million in one year; at four francs, 28 million; at eight francs, 56 million. This is not at all whimsical. There are some well-off workers, and above all, many with generous souls. Some will give two francs, others four, eight, ten or twenty. And just think of how many you are, seven or eight million!

Now let us examine the results **the Worker's Union** could have.

I have just shown that it is not at all impossible for seven million workers; unite in this concept, **to serve their cause and their own interests**. Through voluntary contributions, they could collect 15, 20, 30, 40 or 50 million francs a year. Applied to the gears of a huge machine like the government, 20-50 million is hardly anything; but applied toward a specific object and used carefully, economically, and intelligently, 20-50 million represents enormous wealth. I have stated that with this capital the Worker's Union could acquire true power, the one money grants. Let us see how:

What is the social position of the French working class today, and what rights remain to be demanded?

Theoretically, the organic law ruling French society since the Declaration of the Rights of Man in 1791 is the highest expression of justice and equity. For this law is the solemn recognition legitimizing the holiness of the principle of absolute equality, and not only that equality under God claimed by Christ, but that living equality practiced in the name of body and soul in humanity.

Workers, do you want to know what your rights are in theory? Open the law book governing French society and you will see:

"Art. 1. The French people are equal before the law, regardless of their title or rank.

"Art. 2. In proportion to their wealth, they indiscriminately contribute to the State.

"Art. 3. They all have equal opportunity for civil and military employment.

"Art. 4. Their individual freedom is equally guaranteed; a person cannot be pursued or arrested except under law, in the form prescribed by law.

"Art. 8. All property is inviolable not excepting any called national, as the law does not discriminate among them."

"In fact, according to the spirit and the letter of the Charter's articles, the French worker has no claims with respect to be citizen's and man's dignity. From the Charter's standpoint, his social position is as desirable as he could want. By virtue of the recognized principle, he enjoys

absolute equality, complete freedom of thought, and the guarantee of security for his person and property. What more can he ask? But, let us hasten to say that to enjoy equality and freedom *in theory* is to live *in spirit*. And if he who brought the law of the spirit to the world spoke wisely, "Man cannot live by bread alone," I believe it is also wise to say, "Man does not live **in spirit** alone."

"Reading the 1830 Charter, one is struck by a serious omission. Our constitutional legislators forgot that preceding the rights of man and the citizen, there is an imperious, imprescriptible right engendering all the others, *the right to live*. Now, for the poor worker who possesses no land, shelter, capital, absolutely nothing **except his hands, the rights of man and the citizen are of no value if his right to live** is not recognized first of all (and in this case they are even bitterly derisory). For the worker, **the right to live is the right to work**, the only right that can give him the possibility of *eating*, and thus, *of living*.

The first of the rights that every being enjoys by being born is precisely the one they forgot to inscribe in the Charter. This first right has yet to be proclaimed.

"Today the working class must be concerned with this single claim, because it is based on the strictest equity. And anything short of granting this claim is an abrogation of fundamental rights. So, what is to be demanded?"

THE RIGHT TO WORK

"The working class's own property and the only one it can ever possess are its hands. Yes, **its hands**. That is its patrimony, its sole wealth. **Its hands are the only work tools it has.** Therefore they constitute its **property**, and I do not think its **legitimacy** or utility can be denied. For if the earth produces, it is thanks to manual labor.

To deny that the worker's hands are his property is to refuse to understand the **spirit** of Article 8 of the Charter. Yet this property is uncontestable and, as soon as it comes under discussion, there will be a unanimous voice in support of it. To guarantee the working class's property (as Art. 8 indicates), this right and its free enjoyment must be recognized in principle (as well as in reality). Now, the exercise of this **free enjoyment of property** would consist in being able to use its hands when and how it pleases. And for that, it must have the *right to work*. So the guarantee of this property consists in a wise and equitable *organization of labor*.

The working class thus has two important demands to make:

1.—*The right to work*
2.—*The right to organize*".

Flora insists in her projections as a way to insert in the brain, in the sensibility, and the anguish of the working class the postulates that she formulated; thus, giving priority to the MEN AND WOMEN WORKERS UNION. Only under these postulates would be possible to realize the social structure that will convert the working class in the proprietor of their own destiny; likewise, changing their actual condition of total insecurity and misery, that were not included in the charts from 1789 and 1830.

Flora continues accumulating evidence to reveal the enormous value of the union of the ones that chase a goal. In the revolution of 1979, with the take of La Bastille, the fledging bourgeoisie society gained their freedom from the feudal power that oppresses them. This powerful dynamic gave rise to a new society under their lead. The bourgeoisie held a long and gruesome fight against the nobility for the triumph of their rights, involving the masses in their battles, and deceiving them to believe that they would benefit from displacing the oppressing caste. In reality, the bourgeoisie was the brains and the people were the executing arms, but once the first ones got to power, the people did not get anything in their favor.

Flora says to them: "The bourgeois class has been ESTABLISHED since 1789. Note what strength a body united in the same interest can have. As soon as this class is recognized, it becomes so powerful that it can exclusively take over all the country's powers. Finally in 1830 its power reaches its peak, and without being the least bit troubled by what might occur, it pronounces the fall of France's reigning king. It chooses its own king, proceeds to elect him without consulting the rest of the nation, and finally, being actually sovereign, it takes the lead in business and governs the country as it pleases.

"This bourgeois-owners class represents itself in the legislature and before the nation, not to defend its own interests, for no one threatens them, but to impose its conditions and commands upon 25 million proletarians. In a word, it is both counsel and judge, just like the feudal lords it triumphed over. Being capitalists, the bourgeois make laws with regard to the commodities they have to sell, and thereby regulate, as they will, the prices of wine, meat, and even the people's bread.

"You see, already more numerous and useful, the bourgeoisie has succeeded the nobility. The UNIFICATION OF THE WORKING CLASS now remains to be accomplished. In turn, the workers, the vital part of the nation, must create a huge UNION TO ASSERT THE UNITY! Then, the working class will be strong; then it will be able to make itself heard, to demand from the bourgeois gentleman its RIGHT TO WORK AND TO ORGANIZE.

"The advantage all large constitutional bodies enjoy is the ability to count for something in the State, and in this way, is represented. Today, the ROYALIST UNION has its representative in the Chamber, with its delegate before the nation to defend its interest, its defender being the most eloquent man in France—Monsieur Berryer. THE COLONIAL UNION has its representatives in the Chamber, with its delegates before the motherland to defend its interest. Well, once assembled in body, why wouldn't the working class have its representative before the legislature and nation to defend its interests? Indeed, in number and importance it equals at least the Royalist group and the body of colonial landowners.

Workers, think about this: the first thing you have to do is *to get yourselves represented before the nation*.

"I stated above that the Worker's Union would enjoy real power, that of money. In fact, it will be easy to allocate 500,000 francs a year out of 20 or 30 million to support generously a defender worthy of serving the cause. We cannot doubt that in beautiful, generous, chivalrous France, men of O'Connell's [1] dedication and talent will be found. So if the Workers' Union is well aware of its position and true interests, its first act must be a solemn appeal to men who feel enough love, strength, courage, and talent to dare take on the defense of the most sacred of causes—the workers—.

"Who knows yet what France has in the way of generous hearts and capable men? Who can foresee the effect produced by an appeal made in the name of seven million workers demanding THE RIGHT TO WORK?

Poor, isolated workers, you count for nothing in the nation. But as soon as the WORKER'S UNION is established, the working class will become a powerful and respectable body; and men of the highest merit will court the honour of being chosen to defend it.

"Should the Union be formed in the near future, let us take a quick look at the men who have shown sympathy for the working class, and see who would be the most capable

---

[1] Daniel O' Connell was the most famous defender of Ireland's independence from England. He was their representative before the House of Commons. Ireland paid him an important salary and the many benefits he received for it were considered a subsidy to its best defender. The Irish paid contributions in order to subsidize their defender. Flora always refers to this example, and to the miserable lives of the Irish in their fight against Irish oppression.

of serving this sacred cause. Let us adopt a humanitarian point of view, and since we are looking for men of love and intelligence, let us not consider their religious and political opinions. Besides, the Union's trustee need not be concerned with either political or religious questions. His mission will be limited to drawing public attention to two points: THE RIGHT TO WORK and LABOUR ORGANIZATION for **everyone's well-being"**.

Flora cites many other names from the group of the so called Utopists, Fourierists, and Saint-Simonists, all of whom had been defenders of the working class: Pierre Leroux, Jean Reynaud, Olinde Rodriguez, Constantin Pecqueur, Alphonse de Lamartine, Hippolyte Carnot, Robert de Lamennais, Alexandre Auguste Ledru-Rollin, Gustave Beaumont, Louis Blanc, Prosper Enfantin; they were devoted to the people or aware of how to serve them effectively.

Flora says: "Manual labour has always been and is still looked down upon. The only opinion in this regard is to consider manual labour degrading, shameful, and almost dishonorable for the one engaged in it. This is so true that the worker hides his laboring situation as much as he can, because he himself is humiliated. He who works with his hands sees himself disdainfully cast aside everywhere; this prejudice has infiltrate the customs of all peoples and is even found in their languages. Well, it must be agreed that in face of such a state of things, Prosper Enfantin has shown great strength and superiority in teaching his disciples to honor manual labour. After establishing the law, he wanted to enforce it. So with the superior authority vested in him by his title of religious leader, he required his disciples to work with their hands, to mix among the workers, and to join them in the roughest and most repulsive trades".

Flora says "It is in name of science, and so—called exact science—mathematics—that Victor Considerant, Fourier's foremost disciple, distinguished author, demands the right to work and to organize as the *only* means left to society for salvation. Considerant possesses a science through which he believes he can *harmonically* organize our whole globe. He claims it necessary to begin by organizing labour and granting everyone he right to work. This man of science proceeds from his science and not from his heart. Nevertheless, he could offer some great advantages. Considerant is active; he speaks with spirit and great scientific conviction; and he writes the same way. Moreover, he has been able to position himself to be heard by men in government.

"If Considerant were chosen by the Union, he could acquire considerable importance, which would put him in a position to serve powerfully the interests of the sacred cause.

"Given the importance of the goal, I think it in the interest of the Worker's Union to pay him very generously; for example, 200,000, 300,000, or maybe even 500,000 francs a year. "But, "it will be objected, "Do you think there is a man in France who would dare accept such a huge amount taken from the small voluntary contributions made by the poor workers? Wouldn't he be afraid of being accused, like O'Connell, of selling his dedication to people?"

"It is understandable that O'Connell's political enemies should adopt the tactic of heaping reproaches, insults, and slander upon him over the wages he receives from Ireland. Motivated by partisan hatred, the British aristocracy would like to defame O'Connell in the minds of the Irish to rid Ireland of its defender. Yet O'Connell behavior is nothing but very loyal, legal, and in complete conformity with the rules established by a healthy morality.

"You workers who earn a living by the sweat of your brow, don't you understand that all work deserves pay? Why shouldn't O'Connell, who works to bring Ireland out of slavery, receive the salary earned by his work? And what hard labour it is when a man gives his whole life to the defense of the popular cause! No more repose for him, as he is constantly preoccupied with seeking means of defense; day and night, he is always at work. What about the two million he receives? Can the life of the heart, the soul, and the mind be paid in gold? It is about time to remunerate services according to their usefulness.

"Now, in order to achieve power in our day and age, publicity [1] is needed says, and publicity in all its forms requires money, a lot of money . . . Think of how he will need to have recourse to all means of publicity, through writing (printing costs), through the writing of others (commissions), through the press (advertising costs), through trips to all the tows in France (travel expenses), through the arts (drawing, engraving, lithography costs, etc.), through entertaining society (domestic expenses), and finally propagation by all ways possible: expenses of all kinds.

"Think of how your defender, besides all his other qualities, must be a clever man. He will tactfully have to seize every means available to him to enlist supporters; and to be able to do so intelligently and on a large scale, he will need a lot of money. To maintain his property

---

[1] It would seem incredible that Flora placed emphasis on the idea of **publicity** and all of its aspects to reach public attention. Publicity is a modern term that not has been used in the way that she claimed it in 1843. Nevertheless, her expressions are so realistic that it is surprising that someone as Flora expressed them. She did so in such a way that her shrewdness and knowledge of reality awakened curiosity.

above suspicion, at the end of each year the defender will account to the central committee for his use of funds; and if it is discovered that he has spent in his private interest, his mandate will be revoked".

PLAN FOR THE UNIVERSAL UNIONIZATION OF WORKING MEN AND WOMEN

In the IV Chapter of the Workers Union, Flora tries to sketch the structure of a project, undoubtedly trying to make more accessible the process to follow to the workers level of thought, since the majority of them were illiterate. In spite of her faith on the results she knew it was very difficult.

Flora has used many examples and arguments, and above all, her own experience that has nourished her with the suffering of the working class from France, England and all the countries that she has peregrinated. She never neglected the cause that took her to the marginal neighbours, the slums, the factories, shops where thousands or men women and children cried, subjected to the most heartless exploitation. She has confirmed that men and women, void of any protection for their lives, or health, with miserable salaries and victims or sicknesses produced by the polluted air from the work places, would die on the streets without a Good Samaritan to give them the slightest help. Many times she heard the disgust phrase: "Drunkards" . . . which in many cases were not true, but the tiredness, hunger, or sickness would break their strength. It was the necessary to create shelters, where the workers, elders and children could be looked after without risking their physical integrity or their lives.

For these and all other reasons that she knows about, the sacrificed lives of the workers, are that she thinks of the Palaces. These places will not be merely hospitals, not temporary shelters for homeless. They will be places where social assistance be offered, according to her, to the sick, to the wounded from work accidents, to the women exposed to the so many work hazards, and to the children that wander the streets, begging, while their mothers perform their duties of their long labour schedule.

The Palaces have other functions: to educate the children, shelter the elders that cannot work, to offer a peaceful refuge and offer women a place where they can better their education. She says again and again that women education is the base for the moral and skillful formation of their children.

For these reasons the PALACES are an important part of her projected WORKERS UNION; they are a complement and incentive to make of them an instrument for improvement, able to liberate the most useful and abandoned class from the consequences of exploitation and misery.

She elaborates: "I am going to provide a quick glimpse of the steps to be followed if one wishes promptly to consolidate the Worker's Union on a solid footing.

"Let it be understood that I am not claiming to trace a definitive, unalterable plan. A plan totally spelled out in advance can never be realized. Only in the process can one appreciate the most appropriate means to achieve the enterprise's success. To shape, cut back and affirm in theory only imply to me extreme unawareness of the difficulties of implementation.

"However, as it is natural for the person who conceived of an idea to grasp its entire scope and understand all its ramifications, I believe I must pose some guidelines to alleviate many difficulties and to help set up the *Worker's Union*.

"In order to locate more readily the paragraphs that might have to be consulted, I have decided to number them. This format will appear perhaps a bit strange for I do not mean to list statutes here: just as for the rest of the work, I hereby entreat the reader not to forget that I had to, and in fact did, focus on the content. I felt that in order to treat such issues well, I had to limit myself to being clear and concise, and shy away from certain stylistic effects; formal elegance would have detracted from my subject.

"Wanting to convince, I had to use logic; and logic is the sworn enemy of so-called poetic form. This is why I carefully avoided using a pleasing form which, in the long run, does not prove anything, and leaves the reader enchanted but not convinced.

"To make my idea clearer, I am dividing the plan's outline into parts, with a summary at the beginning so the principal points can be grasped at a glance.

SUMMARY

A. How the Workers Must Proceed to Establish the Worker's Union.

B. How the Worker's Union must proceed from the Financial Point of View.

C. The Intellectual Point of View.

D. On the Use of Funds.

E. Building the Palaces.

F. Conditions for Admission to the Palaces for the Elderly, the Disabled, and Children.

G. Labor Organization in the Palaces.

H. Moral, Intellectual, and Vocational Instruction to Be Given to the Children.

I. The Inevitable Results of This Education.

"1. In their respective trade, union, or welfare groups, the workers must begin by forming one or several committees (according to the number of members) composed of seven members (five men and two women), chosen from the most capable.

"2. These committees may not receive any contributions. Their function will be temporarily limited to inscribing in a great register book the sex, age, names, addresses, and occupations of all those who want to become members of the Workers' Union, and the amount each pledges to contribute.

Flora insists that "by working man or woman, we mean any individual who works with his or her hands in any fashion. Thus, servants, porters, messengers, laborers, and all the so-called odd-jobbers will be considered workers. Only soldiers and sailors will have to be exempted. Here are the reasons for this exception: (a) the State comes to the aid of soldiers and sailors through the disabled fund; (b) and the soldiers are knowledgeable only in destructive work and the sailor in sea work, so neither would be usefully employed in the Worker's Union palace. Since the soldiers and sailors belong to the working-class and by this reason have the right to adhere to the Worker's Union, they will be inscribed separately as brothers. They may contribute toward their children's admission to the palaces.

"In view of the Union, and this is of the utmost importance, the workers must make it their duty and mission to use all their influence to get their mothers, wives, sisters, daughters, and girl friends to join in with them. They themselves must urge them and escort them to the committee so that they can enter their names in the Union's great-book. That is a proper mission for the workers.

"As soon as the working men and women are represented by the committee they will have elected, these committees will then elect a central committee from among themselves for all of France. Its headquarters will be in Paris or Lyons (in the city with the most workers).

"It is agreed that not all of the working-class must be represented by committees in order to nominate the central committee. Thus for Paris, it suffices for an adequate number of working men and women to be represented in order to proceed to electing the central committee. Once the central committee is elected, the Worker's Union will be established.

"It is urgent that the palace be fed by lots of water in order always to maintain strict cleanliness. The palace architecture must be noble but simple. With its high style and ornamental beauty, it must present an aesthetic whole, harmonious in all its parts. The architect must constantly keep in mind that the children raised in these palaces are destined someday to build palaces themselves to house humankind, that they are to become artist—artisans, and that a young age their hearts, imaginations, and senses must be impressed to attain that goal". Flora details all and every one of the particulars to be realized for the completion of the organization itself. She makes sure nothing escapes the most minimal recommendation, so that workers that are not used to institutions of this nature do not make mistakes, as she explains in this chapter, even if they do not use resources that are more expedient. The most fundamental is the constitution of the Workers Union, and for this purpose she counsels what to her own criteria is most useful to obtain the best results.

Flora makes a tally of all the labour institutions that exist in Paris and the whole France, which to rely with for the formation of the respective committees. She as well adds the amounts that would be accumulated from the monthly contributions from the affiliated workers, which would be used to build the Workers Palaces, and deliver peace and welfare to the great proletariat family.

Her letters are not a plead; humbly they retain her dignity, and merely intend to awaken the dormant sentiments of justice that lives in every human being to recognize the rights of the oppressed.

Flora then writes,

"The elders would enjoy all the deserving services that their age and needs merit, so they can enjoy the health and comfort without restrictive impositions of any kind.

"It is implicit that all men, women and children would carry out several duties, as to not foment idleness and vice, that Flora finds detestable.

"Among the activities of the Palace residents are emphasized the physical exercises for the young ones, and the recreation activities that aim to distract and entertain; likewise, the progressive instruction to women and children.

"These are activities for the healthy. For the weak, sick, injured at work, or affected by poor health, the Palaces would have a hospital wing, where they would be rehabilitated by the medical services that they would be fitted with.

She continues, "As soon as the defender is appointed, the central committee must appeal to the King of France, as head of State; to the members of the Catholic clergy, as the leaders of a religion base on a truly democratic principle;

to the nobility, as the most generous and charitable in the nation; to the manufacturers, as indebted to the workers for their fortunes; to the financiers, as indebted to the workers for their wealth, as the workers' labour has made the financiers' money worth something; to the landowners, as indebted to the workers whose labour has made their land valuable; and finally to the bourgeois, too, who lived off and get rich by the labour of the workers.

"If the Workers Union wants create free men and women, the children must be taught to show great respect for human dignity in all aspects of life. To insure this respect, they must be taught never to harm or insult another and never to allow the least injustice or slightest insult, either on the part of their peers or on the part of their superiors. To make this more emphatic, I would like everything in the settlement to be spelled out in written laws and regulations so that the rights and duties of each would be clearly and precisely defined.

She continues: "The results the Worker's Union ought to have are immeasurable. This UNION is a bridge erected between a dying civilization and the harmonious social order foreseen by superior minds. First of all, it will bring about the rehabilitation of manual labour diminished by thousands of years of slavery. And this is a capital point.

As soon as it is no longer dishonorable to work with one's hands, when work is even an honorable deed, the rich and the poor alike will work. For idleness are both a torture for mankind and the cause of its ills.

"I stop here, wanting to leave my readers the sweet joy of counting for themselves the important and magnificent results the Worker's Union will doubtless obtain. In this institution the country will find elements **of order, prosperity, wealth, morality, and happiness, such as they can be desired".**

SUMMARY OF THE IDEAS IN THIS BOOK,
THE GOALS OF WHICH ARE:

1. Consolidation of the working class by means of a tight, solid, and indissoluble Union.
2. Representation of the working class before the nation through a defender chosen and paid by the Worker's Union, so that the working class's need to exist and the other classes' need to accept it become evident.
3. Recognition of one's hands as legitimate property. (In France 25,000,000 proletarians have their hands as their only asset.)
4. Recognition of the legitimacy of the right to work for all men and women.
5. Recognition of the legitimacy of the right to moral, intellectual, and vocational education for all boys and girls.
6. Examination of the possibility of labour organizing in the current social state.
7. Construction of Worker's Union PALACES in every department, in which working-class children would receive intellectual and vocational instruction, and to which the infirm and elderly as well as workers injured on the job would be admitted.

8. Recognition of the urgent necessity of giving moral, intellectual, and vocational education to the women of the masses so that they can become the moral agents for the men of the masses.

9. Recognition in principle of equal rights for men and women as the sole means of UNIFYING HUMANKIND.

THE WORKER'S UNION MARSEILLAISE

Glory to work, glory to love
Through which all men are brothers,
And may heaven hasten the day
For our worker's rights!
Let us unite; in unity
Will disappear our slavery,
And from disinherited people
We will be reborn a wise people!

Old flags, tossed by the winds of chance,
Give in to the unity that founds
And you, Christ's spirit, under the same banner
Rally the soldiers of the world!

Surge forth, noble defender,
Magnanimous and powerful brother,
You, a leader without fear, will make
The faiths motivating us speak!
Interpreter of our hundred voices,
To the tribunal of France
Ascend: and demanding our rights,
Immortalize your eloquence!

Old flags, etc.

Slumber amidst the vanities,
Thesauruses of power,
Without attacking your liberties,
We proclaim our alliance.
Come! Your sumptuous palaces
Will lack the stony brilliance
Of the majestic monuments,
Palaces of the working class!
Old flags, etc.

All our rights of man are yours,
Oh, mothers of humanity,
On your faces as on ours is needed
The sun of equality!
Upon this new world star
Place your triumphant gaze,
Oh, women, the fecund blood
Is attested by your children!

Old flags, etc.

Author
LE CLAIR, student

APPENDIX

UNITED NATIONS

CONVENTION
ON THE ELIMINATION
OF ALL FORMS OF
DISCRIMINATION
AGAINST WOMEN

> *". . . the full and complete development of a country,*
> *the welfare of the world and the cause of peace require*
> *the maximum participation of women on equal terms*
> *with men in all fields."*

UNITED NATIONS

The Convention on the Elimination of All Forms of Discrimination against Women (CEDAW), adopted in 1979 by the UN General Assembly, is often described as an international bill of rights for women. Consisting of a preamble and 30 articles, it defines what constitutes discrimination against women and sets up an agenda for national action to end such discrimination. The Convention defines discrimination against women as "…any distinction, exclusion or restriction made on the basis of sex which has the effect or purpose of impairing or nullifying the recognition, enjoyment or exercise by women, irrespective of their marital status, on a basis of equality of men and women, of human rights and fundamental freedoms in the political, economic, social, cultural, civil or any other field."

Considering that one of the purposes of the United Nations is to promote universal respect for human rights and fundamental freedoms without distinction of any kind, including any distinction as to sex.

Taking into account the conventions, resolutions, declarations, and recommendations to eliminate all forms of discrimination and to promote equal rights for men and women.

Considering that discrimination against women is incompatible with human dignity and the welfare of society and constitutes an obstacle to the full realization of the potentialities of women.

Affirming that women and men should participate and contribute on a basis of equality in the social, economic and political processes of development and should share equally in improved conditions of life.

Determined to implement the principles set forth in the Declaration on the Elimination of Discrimination against women and, for that purpose, to adopt the measures required for the elimination of such discrimination in all forms and manifestations.

States parties shall take all appropriate measures to eliminate discrimination against women in order to ensure to them equal rights with men in the field of education and in particular to ensure, on a basis of equality of men and women. To ensure that family education includes a proper understanding of maternity as a social function and the recognition of the common responsibility of men and women in the upbringing and development of their children, it being understood that the interest of the children is the primordial consideration on all cases.

In order to prevent discrimination against women on the grounds of marriage or maternity and to ensure their effective right to work. To prohibit dismissed on the grounds of pregnancy or of maternity leave.

States parties shall accord to women equality with men before the law, access to health care services including those related to family planning.

States parties shall take into account the particular problems faced by rural women and the significant roles which rural women play in the economic survival of their families.

The Convention shall be established a committee on the Elimination of Discrimination against women.

The Convention shall be open for signature . . .

Shall enter into force on the thirtieth day after the day of deposit with the Secretary General of the United Nations of the twentieth instrument of ratification or accession.

By accepting the Convention, States commit themselves to undertake a series of measures to end discrimination against women in all forms, including:

To incorporate the principle of equality of men and women in their legal system, abolish all discriminatory laws and adopt appropriate ones prohibiting discrimination against women;

To establish tribunals and other public institutions to ensure the effective protection of women against discrimination; and

To ensure elimination of all acts of discrimination against women by persons, organizations or enterprises.

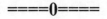

MILESTONES TOWARDS EMANCIPATION
OF WOMEN

1691 UNITED STATES, women have the vote in the State of Massachusetts. They later lost this right in 1780.

1788 FRANCE, the French philosopher and politician Condorcet demands for women the right to education, to participate in politics, and to employment.

1792 UNITED KINGDOM, the pioneer feminist Mary Wollstonecraft publishes "A Vindication of the Rights of Woman".

1840 UNITED STATES, Lucretia Mott founds an "Equal Rights Association", demanding equal rights for women and blacks.

1843 *Flora **Tristan published her book L' Union Ouvrier —The Workers' Union—***

1857 UNITED STATES, March 8, strike of New York women garment and textile workers demanding equal pay and a reduced 10-hour working day. 146 women were killed.

1859 RUSSIA, emergence of a women's emancipation movement in St. Petersburg.

1862 SWEDEN, women given the vote in municipal elections.

1865 GERMANY, Louise Otto founds the General Association of German Women.

1866 UNITED KINGDOM, the philosopher and economist John Stuart Mill calls for votes for women.

1868 UNITED KINGDOM, foundation of the National Women's Suffrage Society.

1869 UNITED STATES, setting up of the National Woman Suffrage Association. State of Wyoming grants women the vote so as to have the necessary quota of electors to qualify for admission to the Union.

1870 SWEDEN and FRANCE open medical studies to women. TURKEY, Inauguration of a college for the training of women primary and secondary teachers for girls' schools.

1874 JAPAN, first teacher training college for girls opened.

1878 RUSSIA, the first women's university opens in St. Petersburg-Bestuzhev University-.

1882 FRANCE, November: a "Ligue pour le droit de la femme" (League for Women's Rights) set up under the patronage of the celebrated author Victor Hugo.

1888 UNITED STATES, Susan B. Anthony founds the U.S. National Council of Women. International Council of Women set up at Washington D.C. by feminist organizations of Europe and North America.

1889 RUSSIA, the famous woman mathematician Sofya Kovalevskaya elected as corresponding member of the Russian Academy of Sciences.

1893 NEW ZEALAND, women obtain the vote.

1901 FRANCE, on a motion by socialist deputy René Viviani, the French parliament discusses women's right to vote for the first time. NORWAY, women begin to vote in municipal elections.

1903 UNITED KINGDOM, Emmeline Pankhurst founds the National Women's Social and Political Union (WSPU).

1904 UNITED STATES, International Woman Suffrage Alliance founded. Feminist meeting in Manchester; Annie Kenney and Christabel Pankhurst arrested.

1906 FINLAND, women granted the right to vote.

1908 UNITED KINGDOM, establishment of the Women's Freedom League. Feminist demonstrations at the Albert Hall and Hyde Park. Emmeline and

Christabel Pankhurst and Flora Drummond jailed after Trafalgar Square meeting.

1910 DENMARK, at the second World Congress of Socialist Women in Copenhagen, Clara Zetkin proposes that March 8 should be chosen as International Women's Day to commemorate the New York women textile workers' strike (March 8, 1857).

1911 JAPAN, creation of the Seito Sha Women's Liberation Movement.

1912 CHINA, several feminist organizations meet in Nanking on January 22, to form an alliance to co-ordinate their activities. They demand equal rights with men and present a petition to Sun Yat-sen, President of the Chinese Republic, on May 20.

1913 NORWAY, equal voting rights achieved by women. GERMANY, AUSTRIA, SWITZERLAND, DENMARK

March 8, women celebrate International Women's Day, demanding the right to vote and to be elected.

1914 TURKEY, first faculty for girls in Istanbul University is created.

1915 SWEDEN, the writer Ellen Key demands that information on birth control be made available and welfare provisions be made for unmarried mothers.

Suffragettes demonstrate in the London streets in 1913, carrying posters in French, German and English, to protest against discrimination.

1917 NETHERLANDS and RUSSIA, women obtain the vote. SOVIET RUSSIA, the October Revolution proclaims and the first Soviet Constitution (1918) confirms the political, economic and cultural equality of women.

1919 UNITED KINGDOM, women over 30 get the vote and the right to sit in Parliament.

1919 GERMANY and CZECHOSLOVAKIA, women given the right a vote.

1920 UNITED STATES, women obtain the vote in all States.

1923 LATIN AMERICA, on April 26, a historic resolution on Women's Rights is adopted during the fifth International Conference of American States in Santiago, Chile.

1925 TURKEY, spectacular progress towards Women's Emancipation follows Kemal Ataturk's election as President.
JAPAN, women are excluded from the "universal" suffrage bill voted by the Diet on March 30. This sparks off the rise of a Japanese Feminist Movement.

INDIA, Poet Sarojini Naidu, a /staunch/ defender of India's feminist movements, elected President of the Indian National Congress.

LATIN AMERICA, Inter-American Women's Commission set up during the sixth International Conference of American States in Havana.

1929 ECUADOR, women obtain the vote.

1932 SPAIN, the Republican Constitution grants voting rights to women.

1934 FRANCE, International Congress of Women for the struggle against fascism and war held in Paris.

1936 FRANCE, three women, including Nobel Prize—winning physicist—Irène Joliot-Curie, enter Léon Blum's Popular Front government although women still not entitled to vote.

1945 FRANCE and ITALY, vote extended to women.

1946 JAPAN. Six women elected to the parliament.

1951 INTERNATIONAL LABOUR ORGANIZATION, the I.L.O. adopts the Convention on Equal Remuneration for Men and Women Workers for work of equal value.

1952 UNITED NATIONS, December 20: United Nations General Assembly adopts Convention on the Political Rights of Women by a big majority.

1956 Peru, vote extended to women.

1957 TUNISIA, a new law affirms equality of men's and women's civil rights.

1959 CEYLON (now Sri Lanka) Mrs. Sirimavo Bandaranaike becomes the world's first woman prime minister.

1961 PARAGUAY, grants voting rights to women. Women can now vote throughout Latin America.

1962 ALGERIA, thirteen women deputies elected to the National Assembly.

1964 PAKISTAN, for the first time a woman. Miss Fatimah Jinnah, stands as a candidate in the presidential election.

1967 IRAN. The "Family Protection Law" allows women to work without their husbands' authorization. Iranian women had been forbidden to wear the veil since 1963.

1971 SWITZERLAND, women get the vote.

1975 UNITED NATIONS, International Women's Year. CUBA, March 8, a "family code" comes into force, requiring Cuban Men to help their wives with the housework.

—0—

BIBLIOGRAPHY ABOUT FLORA TRISTAN

Lewis L. Lorwin. "Historia del Internacionalismo Obrero", Biblioteca Ercilla, 2 tomos. Tomo 1, Cap. IV 1934, págs. 28 sgtes.

Margaret Goldsmith. "Cinco Mujeres Contra el Mundo", 1937, Paris

Ventura García Calderón. "Vale un Perú", 'Nuestra Santa Aventurera' págs. 151-162, Paris, 1939

Samuel Berstein. "Marx en Paris". 1848, ed. 1939

Luis A. Sánchez. "Una Mujer Sola Contra el Mundo". Buenos Aires, Edit. ALA, 1942

Magda Portal. "Flora Tristan, Precursora", Conferencia. Santiago de Chile, 1944; 2a edición, Lima, 1945

G.D.H. Cole. "Historia del Pensamiento Socialista", 7 Tomos; tomo 1 'Los Precursores 1789-1850' Fondo de Cultura Económica, 1962

Dominique Desanti. "Flora Tristan la Revolucionaria", Librería Hachet, Paris, 1972

Estuardo Núñez. "Ensayos Escogidos", Biblioteca Peruana, Ediciones Peisa. Lima, 1974

Yolanda Marco. "Unión Obrera", Flora Tristan. Edit. Fontamara, Barcelona, 1977

BIBLIOGRAPHY FROM FLORA TRISTAN
(Published when she was alive)

Necessité de faire un bon accueil aux femmes etrangeres.
Paris, 1836

Peregrination d'une Paria. 2 vol. Paris, 1838

Petition pour le restablissement du divorce. Paris,1838

Lettres de Simon Bolivar. Paris, 1838

Petition pour l'abolition de la peine de mort. Paris, 1838

Mephis ou le Proletaire. Paris, 1838

Promenade dans Londres. Paris, 1840

L'Union Ouvrier. Paris, 1843

(Published after she died)

L'Emancipation de la Femme ou le Testament de la Paria.
Paris, 1945

Le Tour de France, Journal. 1843-1844

Lettres. Paris, 1980

The London Journal of Flora Tristan. London, 1982